No Time for Down Time?

Copyright © 2004 by Ruth Hoskins

ISBN 0-7414-1883-5

Published by:
INFINITY
PUBLISHING.COM
519 West Lancaster Avenue
Haverford, PA 19041-1413
Info@buybooksontheweb.com
www.buybooksontheweb.com
Toll-free (877) BUY BOOK
Local Phone (610) 520-2500
Fax (610) 519-0261

Printed in the United States of America

Printed on Recycled Paper

Published March 2004

No Time for Down Time?

A 100-MPH Woman Tells You
the Secrets of
Making Time for Yourself

*Meditation and other stress management techniques
help integrate the Mind, Body, and Spirit.*

Ruth Hoskins, LCSW, BCD

This book is dedicated to my son Elijah and my father Leonard, two loving people who taught me the meaning of unconditional love.

Contents

Introduction: My Story

When I was 31 years old I was hospitalized. For over three weeks I was fed through a tube. How did that happen at such a young age? For a year prior to the hospitalization I was unhappy about not being able to get pregnant. I became sick with worry and shame. I denied how deeply I was struggling with the emotional pain and loss, but I didn't share my feelings with anyone except my husband. He was supportive, but he too was grieving.

In my grief I went searching for answers, looking for magical cures. I decided that eating a strict vegetarian diet comprised of many dairy products would make me stronger. I didn't know, then, that I was lactose intolerant—allergic to dairy products. Coupled with my anxious emotional state of mind, the excess worsened what had been a simple stomach problem.

Afraid of what the pain in my side was really telling me, I convinced myself that my body was cleansing. I still thought

I could heal myself through what I falsely believed was a healthy diet. But I was in denial. In reality, the combination of poor diet, unacknowledged grief, suppressed anger, and stress about not being able to conceive caused a stomachache to escalate into ulcerated colitis, the major health crisis that finally put me in the hospital.

For three weeks I lay in a hospital bed, unable even to walk to the bathroom. I used a bedpan, and later when I could walk, I pushed a hyper-alimentation machine that was filled with liquid nutrients and attached to my chest down the hospital hall. During my three-week hospital stay, I experienced the consequences of ignoring the signals my body had been telling me to pay attention to.

When I was well again, I came to understand that denial is a powerful defense mechanism that can affect us either positively or negatively. It can either hurt us—as it did me—because we remain in denial too long and problems worsen. Or it can help us by giving us time to evaluate what is happening in our lives. Denial may temporarily ward off uncomfortable feelings, but if we remain in denial too long and refuse to take a look at what is wrong, our health and relationships may suffer. In my situation, the chronic worry about not getting pregnant made me sick, and even though I felt the pain in my side I chose to ignore it.

There are as many examples of people in denial as there are people. For instance, take a look at those who have been diagnosed with hypertension but won't take the medication, follow a prescribed diet, or take time to relax. They continue to race around all day, believing they don't have the time to change their habits by exercising, or following a prescribed diet, or practicing relaxation. By not taking care of themselves, they may eventually have a stroke.

From my experience, both personally and as a psychotherapist, I know that people remain in denial because they think that if they acknowledge what they need to do and then take action, things won't get any better. But as I discovered, it's when we don't acknowledge the problems in our lives or place our attention on what needs to be changed that things can and do spiral out of control.

When I was sick, I denied the pain in my side and the hurt and emotional loss of not being able to have a child. I told myself that tomorrow would be a better day. Things would change for the better. This was magical thinking.

When I was in the hospital I was frightened. None of the medicines were working as quickly as they should. I was not getting better. Then the bottom fell out. I overheard doctors whispering outside the door of my hospital room. They were talking about performing a colostomy on me. I was only 31 years old at the time. I couldn't believe what I was hearing. It was shocking. Up until that point I was so caught up in my own emotional distress that I hadn't realized how serious my condition really was. From the conversation I overheard, I learned that I had not only lost control of my health, but now others were controlling my future. I knew I had to do something, but I couldn't imagine what that something was.

The real turning point for me was when a nurse came into my room and sat down on the bed. "You must help yourself to get well," she said. Imagine hearing that from a medical person in a hospital! I heard her words but they didn't make sense to me. I must help myself to get well?

At first I felt angry with her. I thought she was kidding. She was the nurse. She was supposed to get me well. It was her responsibility to make me better. After the anger passed, however, I thought perhaps there might be some truth to what she said, so I asked her what she meant.

"You keep asking the doctor when you're going to get pregnant," she said. "But the fact that you want to have a child and haven't yet had one is producing so much anxiety and stress and tension in your body that it's making it difficult for you to even believe that you can get over your illness and have a child. You have to help yourself to get well. And I know that you can do it. It's no secret that stress and anxiety can cause a person to get sick. If you want to get well, you have to believe that you can be healthy. Even though right now you don't feel well, soon you must get out of bed and walk down the hall. You have to make an effort on your own behalf. You have to help yourself to get well."

After hearing the doctor's shocking statement about the colostomy and the nurse's words, I knew I had to take a chance and believe her. She was telling me I had to take charge of my health and myself in order to get well.

But I was sick. I lacked energy and stamina, and the last thing I wanted to do was get out of bed and walk down the hall. I didn't believe I had the power to change anything—especially a life-threatening illness. I had tubes feeding me. I was hooked up to a machine. Still, I knew I had to do something.

I kept repeating the nurse's words: "Help yourself get well." I must have said that sentence hundreds of times. Gradually, my thinking and my vision of myself began to change. Slowly, images began to form in my mind. I had vivid memories of when I was strong and healthy, capable, powerful, and in charge of my life. From these memories I made up new images, visualizations of the way I wanted to see myself in the future, strong and well. I also imagined that I was pushing a baby carriage down the street.

It was wishful thinking but it was fun, and it gave me enough energy and hope to get out of bed and do what the nurse said to do: walk down the hall and help myself. Even though I still wanted the nurse to work her magic and make me well, I was beginning to help myself. The more I practiced an affirming belief about myself, the better I felt. I was empowering myself to feel strong again. I discovered that I could respond in a different, positive way to the nightmare that had produced such a negative effect on my health. By acknowledging what was happening and talking to the nurse about not being able to get pregnant, I began to change. Soon I was well enough to go home. I have never had a repeat of the illness—in fact, a few years ago, a doctor told me that no trace of the disease remains in my body.

For more than 30 years since that time, I have taught people how to manage their stress and balance their lives. Meditation and other stress management techniques as I teach to students in business is an effective and easy-to-use stress management tool that you can practice at home or at work. It takes only a few minutes a day and offers a lot of benefit for a small investment of your time.

Meditation is a simple way to build down time into your life. Hence the title of this book, *No Time For Down Time?* So let's get started.

Exercise: The Balance Scale

Measure the degree of balance in your life by completing the following. Use the scale of, Always, Sometimes, and Never.

1. I often feel anxious and stressed.
2. During the day I am often irritated or annoyed at my boss, spouse, or children.
3. I have high expectations about jobs that need to be completed.
4. I feel resentful that I don't have enough time for myself
5. I put off doing things I want to do for myself.
6. I say that I am going to begin an exercise program, but I never make time for it.
7. I bring work home and I resent it.
8. I ignore my favorite hobby.
9. My children and spouse say I don't spend enough time with them.

10. My responsibilities are so overwhelming that
    sometimes I am angry and depressed.

   If you answered Always or Sometimes to more than
three of these questions, then you need to schedule down
time for yourself.

Chapter 1

Are You a 100-MPH Woman?

"More of us are up in the wee morning hours, perhaps as many as in the 19th-century farm days," according to a recent issue of the *Philadelphia Sunday Inquirer* (March 9, 2003). "It is the relentless need to get things done. All over America, alarms are going off at hours once filled with the sound of snoring. Surveys suggest that about 30 percent of women and 40 percent of men are up more or less before 6 a.m."

And people are more stressed than ever before.

Today, people are overworked and overwhelmed. They cannot get everything done that needs doing in a day. There are not enough hours to accomplish all of the things that a person needs, wants, or must do.

Does this sound like a typical morning for you? The kids have to be dressed and ready to catch the bus for school. Then the hurrying begins. Are the lunches made? Is the homework finished and in the book bag in the hallway where it belongs? Was the homework even done at all? No time to think about that. It is time to get ready for the morning commute. Breakfast needs to be made. The dog needs a quick walk. Who will pick up the kids after school? What's for dinner? Honey, we need a quart of milk. Can you get that? Never mind. I'll get it myself. I have to run. I can't be late. My performance review is next week. My raise depends on it. If I leave the house right now I may be able to avoid the jammed tollbooth lines.

Perhaps it's one of those mornings when your teenager decides that he or she won't get out of bed and go to school. Or your toddler isn't cooperating with your schedule. You scream. "Hurry up! Get dressed and get out of bed right now. If you don't..." Here come the threats. Now you try to hoist your 160-pound, 16-year-old teenage boy out of bed, or put a snowsuit on the three-year-old who's sprawled spread-eagled and screaming, arms and legs flailing.

There's no time for uncooperative children. You still have to get yourself ready for work, and yelling isn't helping anybody move any faster. Door slamming, huffing and puffing, stomping down the hall hurling insults doesn't motivate the family either. Besides, this isn't the way you want to start your day. Your face is red. Your blood pressure is rising. Spouse and children dig in their heels or pull the covers over their heads. But you have to run out the door to begin the morning commute anyway.

After driving through jammed bumper-to-bumper traffic, you arrive at work and are greeted by a coworker standing at the entrance to your cubicle, coffee in hand, smiling and ready to chat. But you're here early to complete yesterday's paperwork, and catch-up on emails and phone calls. You're tired of bringing unfinished reports home at night. You don't have time to talk but find it difficult to say no.

You want to be polite. You smile at her the same way that you will smile all day long while interacting with your boss who is asking you to hurry up and finish another project with another deadline. Once again, she is insisting that everything be done today by noon. Today you rushed around and ate lunch sitting at your desk. The 15-minute walk you promised must wait until tomorrow. Again.

On the ride home through rush hour traffic you glance at the papers in your brief case—the ones you didn't want to bring home, but did because you're worried about the rumor mill and the possibility of job cuts. At the day-care center you drive into the parking lot and hurry into the building to pick-up your whiny, sleepy, hungry child. Then you stop at the grocery store to buy that quart of milk. Back in the car, you turn on the radio and if you're lucky, you have a few quiet minutes of down time for yourself before driving home to begin second shift.

At home, your spouse is reclining comfortably in his favorite chair, reading the newspaper. Music blares from your teenager's room. The house is a mess—dishes piled in the sink, coats and book bags everywhere, lights on in every room in the house. Didn't the kids promise that their homework would be done before dinner? Your spouse looks up at you and smiles. But before he can say hello to you, you say to him, "Would you mind putting the newspaper down?" You think to yourself, "I'd like a little time for myself too!"

Today, women work two jobs. It's a fact of life: women are exhausted. Yet we hide the need to close the door and take a quiet warm bubble bath undisturbed. As women, we don't have enough time for our families, let alone for ourselves. We haven't seen our friends in months. But we place our own need for down time last on the to-do list, and we are paying the price.

We have too many roles and jobs and wear dozens of hats and everything is a priority. In the workshops I teach, women (and men too) tell me how busy they are. Everybody works a nine-to-five job that's more like six in the morning to six at night. But the majority of women I meet are still in charge of cooking, cleaning, packing lunches, and making sure homework is done.

Juggling family life and work is challenging, and women today feel out of control, angry, frustrated, and guilty that we aren't the Super Moms we think we ought to be. Our health is compromised. We know our lives are out of balance. And we don't feel psychologically or spiritually nourished.

Ladies, it is time to take off your 100-MPH running shoes and learn to relax. I did it. You can, too.

Chapter 2

The Body's Response to Stress

When we're stressed, blood pressure rises and the production of gastric acid increases to prepare us for a long-haul fight or challenge. Our pupils dilate. Our hearts pump blood faster. Hearing and vision sharpen. Breathing becomes rapid and shallow. Muscles tense. Adrenaline and other hormones rush into the bloodstream to alert us to danger. This physiological stress response prepares us to survive serious confrontation, and that's a good thing—when such a physical confrontation exists. But too much stress just wears us down. And when stress becomes long-term and without relief, it can cause serious illness.

Estimates are that more than 35 million people in the United States suffer from depression. In fact, many people also suffer from migraine or tension headaches, hypertension, ulcers, and other psychological, stress-related disorders. A University of Tennessee study showed that more than half of all hospital admissions could be prevented by simple changes in lifestyle.

A medical journal on cardiology recently reported that negative emotions have a direct effect on the blood flow in the heart. In one study, 132 outpatients wore heart monitors for 48 hours while living their normal lives and writing detailed diaries of their activities and emotional states. Results showed that the negative emotions of anger and frustration more than doubled the risk of unhealthy heart contractions. Unless such negative emotions can be controlled with effective stress management techniques like meditation, stress emergency hormones affect the body and can contribute to disease.

Keep in mind that the way each of us responds to stress is highly individualized. Some stress is motivating. For example, adrenaline can jump-start athletes and give them energy to win the race. But when stress becomes long-term and with no relief or a system to successfully manage it, the effects can be devastating.

But there's hope. Meditation creates balance and helps you get in touch with your inner self, feelings, purpose, and goals. When you make down time just for yourself, even if it's a small amount of time every day, you'll feel better— because plugging in down time with meditation helps control stress. In the August 4, 2003 issue of Time Magazine, "one study, for example, shows that women who meditate and use guided imagery have higher levels of the immune cells known to combat tumors in the breast." And if you can't find a reason to practice meditation for yourself, then do it for the sake of your children. Children sense their parents' emotions and, in response to tension, often experience stress, anger, and unhappiness themselves without knowing the reason why.

The research is in and the facts are clear. Edward Charlesworth and Ronald Nathan in their book, Stress Management, describe stress-related symptoms in three D's. They say that stress creates Disorders. Stress increases the need for Drugs. And stress costs companies and consumers Dollars. They write that 30 million Americans have some form of major heart or blood vessel disease. Each year, Americans spend $5 billion on tranquilizers and American industry loses $19.4 billion because of premature employee death.

It's no secret that we need time for ourselves to relax and reduce stress. The instinct to curl up with a good book, lock the door, and take a hot bath is natural. The need to close our eyes for a few minutes in the afternoon is normal. When people are deprived of a period of quiet, tension and stress increase. Closing our eyes in the middle of the day and relaxing is as necessary to good health as drinking water, eating good foods, getting a good night's sleep, and breathing—and relaxation helps to reduce stress. I believe that we do have at least 15 minutes every day for meditation, a closed eye process, just for ourselves.

Ask yourself these questions. Why am I taking care of everybody else leaving no time for myself? Why do I run from home to job, to picking up children, car pooling, arranging children's social schedules, and leaving no down time for myself? The answer is that you've put yourself last on your own "to do" list.

We're meant to have down time. Meditation gives us the time we need to regroup and re-energize. During meditation we not only let go of stress, but we ask ourselves questions and we listen for answers. We build a relationship between our self and the Higher Self. Having a reasonable amount of quality down time every day—written down in your scheduler just as you'd write down an important meeting on your calendar—is a must for your health and well-being. Without it, your stress levels escalate.

Quick Stress-Reducing Tips

1. **Breathing:** Close your eyes. Put your attention on your breath. Mentally, follow the air in through your nose and down your throat, warming your body. Exhale through your mouth slowly. When your mind wanders, bring your attention back to your breath. Do this anytime, at your desk or at home, for one to three minutes. Then relax naturally.

2. **Mini-Meditation:** Close your eyes. Breathe. Follow the breath, inhaling, exhaling, slowly, telling yourself to relax. Let the word "Relax" come into your mind. The word Relax will drift out of your mind. Let it go. Effortlessly say, "Relax, release. Relax, release. Relax, release." Do this for five minutes at least once a day. Then slowly bring yourself out of the mini-meditation, taking from three to five minutes to do so.

3. **Progressive Relaxation:** Sit comfortably and close your eyes. Begin breathing, inhaling and exhaling, gently and with awareness. Bring your attention to the bottom of your feet. Tighten, then relax your feet. Move your attention up your body to your legs, belly, buttocks, chest, neck, shoulders, arms, face. Gently tighten each part of your body, hold for a few seconds, and then release. Sit quietly. Take from three to five minutes, and then slowly open your eyes.

4. **Visualization/Affirmation:** Close your eyes. Gently, put your attention on your breath. Mentally, follow the air in through nose and down your throat, warming your body, then out again. Effortlessly say Relax, release. Relax, release. Relax, release. Gently, allow a picture to form in your mind. See yourself as relaxed and healthy, prosperous and well. Allow this image of yourself to flow in and out of your mind. Say to yourself, "I am well. I am prosperous. I am healthy. I am whole."

Chapter 3

CPR — Consciously Preparing to Relax

To accept the fact that it's normal to relax every day is to take the first step in reducing stress. The acronym I use to remind clients to relax is "CPR — Consciously Preparing to Relax."

In an emergency situation, the body needs oxygen. When stressed, the body needs oxygen too, to let go of stress and to relax.

To begin relaxation, Conscious Breathing is the simplest stress management technique, and it only takes seconds to do. Conscious breathing helps restore balance and to reduce stress. Even if you don't have one minute to close your eyes and relax, you still can become more deeply conscious of your breathing. Here's how.

Put your hand on your belly and breathe with awareness. Breathe slowly, inhaling and exhaling. Take three deep breaths, pushing out your navel, and relax. Now, stop the exercise. Go back to what you were doing. Wait five minutes and begin again. Put your hand on your belly and breath. Breathe slowly, inhaling and exhaling. Do this three times and then stop and relax.

This simple yet highly effective technique quickly calms the emotions and focuses the mind, helping you to center yourself. Practice the technique by linking it to an activity that you do every day, such as looking at your watch or talking on the telephone. That particular daily activity acts as a reminder for you to breathe consciously.

Our breath is our life. Our life is dependent on our breath. Everyone breathes. But not everyone breathes the same way. Many of us are shallow breathers. We don't breathe from our bellies, filling our lungs with air by bringing the air up our chests. We breathe short, quick, rapid breaths from the upper chest, especially when we're stressed. In fact, when we're upset or confronted with a conflict, we tend to hold our breath and tighten our bodies. Remembering to breathe consciously is an easy and very efficient stress management tool. Pay attention to your breath. Become a conscious breather. You will feel less stressed. Conscious Breathing is the quickest way to get a quick minute of down time in your day.

I use Conscious Breathing whenever I feel anxious, tense, or angry. If I wake up in the middle of the night and feel overly concerned that I won't be able to fall back asleep, I begin to pay attention to my breathing. I consciously inhale and exhale. It relaxes me and I fall asleep.

Before I begin a workshop, I pay attention to my breathing. It helps me feel centered. I love teaching, but when I see a group of one hundred smiling faces staring back at me, my heart beats more rapidly so I begin Conscious Breathing.

The following exercises can be practiced for 10 seconds throughout the day. You may increase the amount of time that you want to do Conscious Breathing, but don't do it if you begin to feel lightheaded. In our society we have a tendency to believe that doing more is better. Being consistent is more important. Conscious Breathing doesn't require much time or a big effort. Build the habit of Conscious Breathing for 10 seconds a day, increasing the exercise to 30 seconds a day. Do this as often in the day as you need.

10-Second Exercise #1:

Sit in a comfortable position. Become conscious of your breath. Take a breath in, filling your lungs and raising your shoulders at the same time. Hold your shoulders up to the count of three. Release the shoulders and the breath at the same time. Now, relax and sit comfortably in your chair. Wait a few seconds and repeat the exercise. Take a breath in and fill your lungs, raising your shoulders at the same time. Hold to the count of three and release the breath and the shoulders at the same time, exhaling through the mouth. Now relax and sit comfortably in your chair.

10-Second Exercise #2:

Become aware of your breathing. Place your hand on your belly and breath. Take a breath in and push the belly out. With the belly extended, hold the breath for a few seconds and then release, relaxing the belly, the hand, and the breath. Breathe normally. Repeat the exercise. Breathe normally.

10-Second Exercise #3:

Take your left thumb and place it on your nose. Close the left nostril with your thumb. With the left nostril closed, breathe in through the right nostril to the count of four. Hold the breath to the count of four. Now, still keeping the left nostril closed, exhale to the count of four. Relax your hand on your lap and breathe normally. Now repeat the exercise using your right hand this time and closing off the right nostril with your thumb. Breathe in through the left nostril to the count of four, hold for four counts, and exhale for four counts.

A variation of alternate nostril breathing is to use one hand, closing a nostril with your thumb, breathing in to the count of four, holding the breath to the count of four, and then exhaling to the count of four. Then with the same hand, releasing that nostril and closing the other nostril with the fingers of the same hand and repeating the exercise to the count of four.

Conscious Breathing Tips

1. Sit in a comfortable position.
2. You may walk around the room.
3. Place either hand on your belly.
4. Become aware of your breathing.
5. Breathe in and out, consciously following the breath through the nose, into the lungs, and out again. Do each step to the count of four.
6. The lungs expand gently and then release the breath consciously and gently.
7. Exhale slowly.
8. Repeat.
9. Begin with 30 seconds and increase to one minute.
10. Avoid getting lightheaded.

Chapter 4

Meditation

"I am a wave of peace."
Paramahansa Yogananda

One of the main benefits of meditation is the deep rest that the mind and the body receive during a 15- to 20-minute session. Practiced daily, an effortless meditation helps prevent new stress from accumulating. Research shows that people who practice meditation like the one that I teach have more energy, clarity of mind, and better health. And it's a simple way to build down time into your day.

In *Brain Power,* authors Vernon H. Mark, M.D., and Jeffrey P. Mark, M.sc., write, "We now know that a stressed, unhappy, and depressed brain makes the body and its defenses more vulnerable. Notice how often the loss of a lifelong spouse causes the surviving partner to become seriously ill, or the death of one partner in a successful marriage will be followed by the death of another."

Meditation helps make the mind and body happy by reducing stress, irritability, and anxiety. Meditation reduces blood pressure. In *Mega Brain*, Michael Hutchison says that meditation increases the capacity of the brain to grow and evolve, "to escape to a higher order of coherence and enriched interneural communication."

Meditation produces slower more powerful brain waves associated with feelings of well-being. A client to whom I taught meditation measured her blood pressure before beginning a session and again after the session. Before the session, her blood pressure was 175 over 121. After one meditation session, her blood pressure was 140 over 101—a significant decrease. A few days later she called to tell me that she was practicing the technique twice a day and was happy to report that her blood pressure had dropped to 120 over 80, or nearly normal. Of course, she continues to take her medication as well.

When we practice an effortless type of meditation, oxygen decreases, suggesting a deep state of rest. During the process our thoughts quiet down. It is not something that we make happen; it's something that, with regular practice, happens automatically. When we turn our consciousness inward, physiological changes take place. We produce alpha waves that suggest a deeper state of rest. Endorphins, the "feel-good hormones," sweep through our bodies. These chemicals, which have been called keys to paradise, are produced during meditation. According to a study completed by Rudestam in the 1980s, "People who meditate claim that it produces a sense of relaxation and well-being. People who meditate believe that it plays a central role in their successful adjustment overcoming the daily stresses and hassles of life."

I have been meditating for over 30 years and I agree with the findings. Also, the people I teach meditation to tell me that they feel calmer, happier, more balanced, and relaxed. It's how they build down time into their days.

Mythical Conceptions of Meditation

People have many myths about meditation. They think they must sit on top of a mountain in a cave with their eyes closed and their legs tucked underneath them, their minds completely blank.

This is a myth. Meditation can be practiced anywhere. It helps to have a quiet space that you can retreat to, but it isn't necessary. You can practice meditation anywhere you can close your eyes—at your desk, on the train, on the bus ride home to and from work. When I was a college student, I meditated in the library because it was quieter than my dorm room. I put on my sunglasses, closed my eyes and began the process, and I have been doing it everyday for 30 years. Meditation has helped me overcome many stressful events. It helps balance my life. It provides a deep rest in the middle of the day, just when I need it the most.

Meditation Tips

1. During meditation you will continue to have thoughts.
2. Thoughts will naturally come and go. This is normal. This is natural. Having thoughts is the correct way to meditate. The reason that we have thoughts while practicing the technique is that it is the nature of the mind to think.
3. Don't expect phenomenal experiences from meditation. It is practiced for the purpose of balancing one's life, releasing stress, and giving the body and mind a deep rest. It's an excellent way to build down time into your day.

People often think that every meditation experience will be exactly the same. Meditation sessions vary. Even after 30 years, I still have days when I just don't feel like sitting down and meditating. I think that I am too busy to take 15 minutes for myself. But the habit is strong so I continue to do it, and I always feel a sense of balance and peace when I finish.

Chapter 5

An Effortless Meditation Technique

In my experience with various meditation techniques, an effortless technique such as the one I teach is the easiest and most beneficial. Other techniques suggest that we concentrate on a word, and this tends to produce some strain and tension in the mind and body. Generally speaking, people won't continue to do a process that produces tension. In my workshops, participants are surprised that they don't have to concentrate and work hard to get benefit. Once again, that has to do with the way our society views success: It has to be hard to get there. But in meditation, success comes by simply doing the process every day.

Here's a summary of the benefits of effortless meditation:

1. Rest for the body and mind.
2. Stress reduction.
3. Anger and tension reduction.

4. Increase in self-confidence, creativity, and clarity of mind.
5. Increase in endorphins associated with feelings of well being.
6 Reduction of cortisol associated with the fight-or-flight response.

Effortless Meditation Session

Sit in a comfortable position in a chair, or lie down on the floor. (If you lie down, you'll probably fall asleep. However, if that's the easiest way for you to learn the technique, then begin doing it that way.)

Now close your eyes. Gently put your attention on your breathing. Consciously follow the breath in, inhaling slowly and exhaling slowly, relaxing. Now allow the word "Relax" to drift into your mind. I use the word Relax because it's easy to remember. When we use a word like Relax, it allows our consciousness to be drawn inwards. It's natural for the word Relax to drift out of your mind again. Don't chase the thought around in your mind; let it go and when you remember to do so again, easily and effortlessly, say the word Relax. As mentioned, in the process of practicing meditation you will have thoughts, but even though you have thoughts you are still meditating. Sometimes our thoughts are quieter. Sometimes they are noisier. When you become aware that you are thinking, say silently, Relax.

A nice way to begin meditation is by bringing your attention to the bottom of your feet. Sitting comfortably, bring your attention to your ankles, your calves, and knees, your thighs and waist, your arms and hands, and tell yourself to relax. Remind yourself that your shoulders are releasing and relaxing, even your face muscles, your ears, eyes, and all the way to the top of your head, relaxing, releasing.

After finishing the 10- to 15-minute meditation session, slowly begin to open your eyes, always taking from 3 to 5 minutes to come out of meditation. Don't rush or jump up from the process. Move slowly. Stretch and let yourself adjust to the light in the room. Enjoy the relaxed feeling.

10-Point Summary
1. Remember that your thoughts will come and go.
2. Allow your thoughts to come and go.
3. Say silently the word Relax
4. The word Relax will fade away.
5. Then it will return again.
6. Sometimes you will fall asleep or drift away. That is okay.
7. Again introduce the word "Relax" into your mind, effortless and easily.
8. Do the technique for 15 to 20 minutes every day.
9. Slowly open your eyes.
10. Take from three to five minutes to come out of meditation.

Chapter 6

Other Beneficial Stress Management Techniques: Letting Go of Guilt and Delegating

Women are multi-taskers. We do many things, wear many hats, and we do our jobs well. We believe, often rightfully, that it's easier not to delegate a task because it just won't get completed the right way. And when we finally do let go and delegate, we spend the time we'd hoped to save looking over someone else's shoulder, micromanaging his or her job. We forget that if we commit to one more job, we have to let go of something else.

Delegating means setting limits and setting healthy boundaries. This is important when we remember that there are 24 hours in a day. We spend at least 8 to 10 hours at work. In that 24-hour period, besides working, we have to sleep, eat, and drive to work, which together take up about eleven more hours. That adds up to 21 hours of time that we must spend just doing the basics in life. We have only four hours left—not much time to do the food shopping, cooking, cleaning, carpooling, and all the other details that make up a day.

In many situations, balancing your life means setting clear boundaries between the three main areas of life: personal, social, and work. For example, if you're aiming for more personal time, then don't bring your laptop home with you or check your email when you're on vacation. However, workshop participants often say they like to do some work on vacation, like checking email. It helps to put out fires at work before they get worse.

Life has indeed changed.

Not long ago, we would never bring laptops or do any work while on vacation. It was a sacred time to relax. Now, even if we choose to leave the laptop at home, the hotel usually has a computer room. Recently, when I went on vacation to the islands, I promised myself that I would not check my email. I left my laptop at home. For three days I kept my promise, but on the fourth day I went to the hotel computer room, logged on to the computer, and checked my email.

The work we do and the people we interact with make us feel good. We find comfort in our work and we like the idea that people need us even when we're on vacation. Today, because of rushed daily schedules, it is even more important to be conscious of keeping our vacation time separate from our work so that vacation time is relaxing. We have to discipline ourselves and learn to say no even to ourselves. An important delegating tip is learning to say no.

Don't say "yes" when you mean "no." And when someone asks you to explain why you can't or won't do a task or why you want to delegate something, be brief. If you over-explain your reasons, you may begin to feel guilty, second-guess yourself, and retract your request. Think about how often people begin a sentence with "Would you mind doing this for me?" and then finish with "Never mind. I can do it myself."

There are always barriers to delegating. One already mentioned is that we think that we're the only ones who can do a task well. Another block to delegating is our need to have the job done the way we would do it. When you delegate a task, there may be flaws in the job, but that's okay. Go back to the person and explain what needs to be changed, but don't micromanage a delegated task. If delegating the task gives you some free time, enjoy it. Sit back, close your eyes, and say the word Relax. Soon, you will drift off into a deep and restful meditation. When you open your eyes again, you'll feel refreshed and renewed. Once you begin to practice meditation you will wonder how you ever lived without it.

Another barrier to delegating is guilt. If you feel guilty about asking for help, or when you do ask for help you wish you hadn't, step back and practice healthy detachment. Healthy detachment helps a person let go of guilt. Remember that guilt is a judgment we place on ourselves. If you keep judging your decisions or if you resist asking for help because of guilty feelings, you're wasting your time. And if you worry constantly about the delegated job or look over someone else's shoulder, afraid of the results, you lose the time you meant to save. Guilt wastes precious time! Instead, congratulate yourself. Pat yourself on the back. Don't minimize what you did by retracting it. You delegated a task. Now let go and relax.

Sometimes we don't delegate because we don't want to be outperformed by others, even members of our own family. Let's get honest: Women like the feeling of being able to juggle many things in a day. It makes us feel competent and in control. But it's time to let someone else do some of the work. Show them how to do the job, step, back, be patient, let go, and relax.

When my son was 11 years old, I wanted him to begin doing his own laundry. We went to the supermarket. Together we chose the laundry detergent. Then I demonstrated to him what I wanted him to do. I didn't point out to him that if he wanted to have clean clothing, he'd have to wash his own laundry. I didn't threaten him. I demonstrated and I delegated.

From that day on he washed his own laundry. He got the message that if he wanted clean clothing, he had to wash, dry, and fold his laundry. The job made him feel competent and gave me some much needed down time.

In reality, everyone in the house can help with household chores. Most young children enjoy earning points for doing their chores. For example, so many points can equal a trip to a store to buy a special toy. Teenagers can earn their privileges this way too, and the sooner you set up an accepted structured system, the better off the family will be during those harder-to-handle teenage years. Hanging a calendar on the refrigerator is an easy and effective tracking system. It reminds parents and children which jobs have been delegated and to whom—and the consequences that have been discussed in a family meeting for jobs that don't get done. Families who delegate household chores in this way value each other and feel strong and connected.

Family meetings are a great way to build in quality time with your children and spouse. Air family concerns and problems. Assign chores. Actively involve your children in these meetings. Value their input. Ask them for their ideas. Tell your children what you plan to do just for yourself this week. Speak your needs and your goals aloud to your family. You'll find this reinforcing. Speaking needs will help you keep commitments. It also lets family members know that you value yourself. Tell them that when you feel rested and relaxed, you're better able to meet family and work demands. Write your name and down time for the week on the family event calendar. It isn't selfish to learn to prioritize yourself at least some of the time—it's practical. Now let go of guilt, put your feet up, close your eyes, and relax.

Tips for Balancing Work, Home, and Life

1. Learn to say "no." You'll have a happier and more balanced life.
2. Let go of what you can't control. You'll gain peace of mind.
3. Take care of yourself every day. Do something special just for you. Take a bubble bath. Read a magazine. Sit down and close your eyes for five minutes. Go for a walk.
4. Think positive thoughts. The way you think is one thing that you do have control over.
5. Compliment yourself during the day as much as possible. Toot your own horn. No one else is going to toot it for you. Say things like "I am doing something special just for me, guilt-free. I like myself. I am happy about my life."
6. Give up the need to be perfect. Forgive yourself for your mistakes.
7. Keep your expectations reasonable. Delegate.
8. Practice Conscious Breathing to oxygenate the body. Imagine fresh, clean, clear air flooding your cells and the organs of your body, making you feel relaxed.
9. When you get upset, count to 10. This helps buy time so that you can respond with self-control.
10. Use "I" statements. Say, "I need time for myself. I need a break." Ask for help. Say, "Can you help?"
11. Dinner doesn't have to be perfect. Sometimes pizza is just fine. The kids will love it.

12. On weekends, cook and freeze microwavable meals for rushed weekday meals.
13. Have regular family meetings. Bring a timer to the meeting and, without interruption, let everyone express his or her feelings for three to five minutes. Write down your expectations about chores and consequences. Get agreement. Post them on the refrigerator.
14. Tell your children and spouse, "When I come in the door after my workday is over, I'm going into my room to relax for 10 minutes." Take a 10-minute break before moving on to the next activity.
15. Keep a magnetized pad and paper on the refrigerator and mark down needed grocery items. Divide the shopping chores. Delegate. Ask, "Can you pick up the milk today and tomorrow too?"

Chapter 7

How I Learned to Set Boundaries and Say "No"

It was 1952 and I was five years old. I remember sitting in the middle of my family's living room on the floor playing with my dollhouse. My sister Nancy was there beside me on the Oriental rug. My parents had divorced; my father was in Spain "on business," my mother told us, mysteriously.

All of a sudden, as in a fairy tale, there came a knock at the front door. A special delivery package had just arrived in the mail from my father, for both my sister and me. These mailed packages were a sign to me that he still cared for us.

Nancy immediately started ripping her present open. Wrapping paper flew around the room. Daddy had sent her a red leather vest with shiny, gold buttons. It took her only three seconds to unwrap her gift, then she took a deep breath, and with that familiar squint in her eye that I remember so well (which usually signaled trouble for me), she said sweetly, "Let me see what you have in there." I slowly peeled off the brown paper from around my present, wanting to savor each precious minute, keeping the memory of my father close to me for as long as I could.

Eventually a matador doll from Spain emerged, nestled in white tissue. I ran my fingers down his black, sequined pants, up and over his red jacket, and across his soft, black felt hat. Then I took the shiny silver sword from around his waist. For a brief moment I held him in my arms. Then, I gave away my doll to my sister, as she had silently requested.

Nancy was the first, but by no means the last, in a long line of people to whom I would give my dearest possessions. I gave away hundreds of things: a new blue Pontiac convertible, a trip to Jamaica, a closet full of fashionable clothes, my dog, even my bank account. Once, I gave my bicycle to a new neighbor boy down the street when he said that he had lost his. The list is endless—so many that I can't remember them all.

Taking care of people at my own expense never mattered to me as long as I was helping "a friend in need." It was no surprise to anyone in my family when they heard I was going to become a social worker.

Over the years, I would eventually work for a hospice, a soup kitchen, and a shelter for runaways. I founded a networking agency that employed professionals to counsel people. I directed a family relationship-counseling agency.

I was the quintessential 100-MPH woman, the one with her life on track. A newspaper article once wrote about me, "She is a woman of energy. She is brave and determined, just like those contemporary pioneers who made the journey across our country paving the way and setting up outposts for those to follow. Ruth is a true Renaissance woman."

In fact, I didn't know how to take care of myself. As a therapist, I understood a woman's pain when she told me she was spending her life taking care of her husband, cooking, cleaning for her children, and leaving no time for herself. I knew this woman: she was me.

At 45, I finally discovered that I gave excessively to other people and often compulsively took care of them as well. I didn't know how to say "no." I discovered the truth about myself when I was married to a man I would have done anything for. I lived to make him happy.

One night, as I was driving back from the supermarket with the fixings for our favorite Saturday night Mexican dinner, I saw him stopped at a traffic light, heading away from our house. I flashed him my brightest smile and hung my head out the car window, yelling at him, all smiles and good cheer.

"Pull over," I hollered gaily. When he reluctantly parked, I climbed into his car beside him. That's when I saw his packed suitcase tossed onto the back seat of the car, the one we had used last month on the trip to Hawaii.

"I left you a note," he said. "I'm leaving."

"Where are you going?" I said, thinking about the fixings for the Mexican dinner in the back seat of my car.

"I am leaving," he said. "Take care of yourself." And that was the end.

When the marriage ended I felt as if someone had died in my arms. At night I paced the floor, and when I finally slept I dreamed I was paralyzed and sprayed with a lethal chemical that controlled my mind and my body. In the dream, I was in great danger of dying. I had to decide whether I wanted to live or to die.

I finally realized that I didn't have a decision to make. I had only one choice: to get better—a choice I had made time and time again. And so I dragged myself up the flight of stairs to my first 12-step Codependents Anonymous recovery meeting.

I sat in this meeting for three years with strangers who eventually became my friends. I took off my mask. For years I had worn the face of Superwoman, healer of all wounds, the 100-MPH Give-Away Woman who gave away too much of herself. I felt a myriad of sensations I had never felt before, including a new one: shame I had buried that one so deeply in my unconscious that for all practical purposes it didn't even exist.

Gradually I learned that, by taking care of people and giving to them, I avoided facing my own painful feelings, memories, and fears. My deepest fear, of course, was abandonment. This I had kept at bay. Instead, I'd imagined that Cinderella and my good, beautiful, and benevolent fairy godmother would wave her sparkling silver wand, and make all bad things disappear. I had believed she would always be there for me, as I was always there for others.

Unlike my mother, who was too busy, I'd made this fairy godmother into the embodiment of perfect love, the perfect woman, and the person I was going to be.

I continued this fantasy up in to my 20s, when I moved into an ashram to worship the guru. He naturally became my new fairy godmother. It was now to him that I gave all things, money as well as love and devotion. Of course, by now this was easy for me. I had become a master at the game of giveaway, for wasn't I the Giveaway Queen? I worshipped at the feet of the guru—at the feet of many good gurus, in fact, and I lived in one ashram after another, seeking truth and fairy godmothers, yet hating the politics, the contention, and the infighting of ashram life. All the while I affirmed my love for everything and felt I was holding my breath, something no one can do for long. One night, with a nagging feeling that could not be washed away no matter how many hours I sat with my eyes closed or my legs tucked underneath me, I left the ashram for good.

As a replacement, I took my fantasies into two marriages. For the seven years of each marriage, and through the illness I'd ignored, I'd believed that God or some omnipotent force (or my fairy godmother) would save me. I kept on giving, and I kept on praying that the pain would go away. It didn't.

In Codependents Anonymous, I began to feel a new set of feelings, and I was able to grieve, a word I hadn't thought applied to me. To ease the ache in my heart from the loss of my second marriage, I went to meetings every day and walked for miles, while memories of people I had taken care of flooded my mind. And I waited for my second husband to return, in much the same way I had waited for my father to return from Spain.

I now believe my second husband did me a great favor by leaving. His abandonment forced me to finally face the fear of being left by someone, and it opened a floodgate of grief. One memory that returned to me was when my mother took my sister and me away from our family home, and left my father a note. I never got to say goodbye to him, but I unconsciously grieved for him, my first love, for 45 years.

Today, I understand the importance of saying "no" and prioritizing myself. I love doing things just for me. Everyday I make a small to-do list. At the top of my list I write, "Today I prioritize the following, just for me." And I always remember to close my eyes and to meditate.

Tip: Practice Saying "No"

Practicing saying no consists of two positive statements followed by a refusal statement. Example: It's eight o'clock in the evening. The PTA chairperson calls and asks you to bake cookies for tomorrow. It would mean so much to the children and to your little Jimmy too, she says.

1. Positive statement # 1: "I love baking cookies for the class."
2. Positive statement # 2: "I enjoy working with you."
3. Refusal statement: "But I don't have the time this evening. Please call again because I love baking cookies for the class."

People can be very persistent and persuasive. Be strong. Hold your ground and remember that if you say yes when you want to say no, the time you scheduled to curl up and read your book tonight will be gone.

Chapter 8

Put Yourself First, At Least Some of the Time

People in my workshops tell me that, for them, everything is a priority.

Life is demanding. And unfortunately, that's not going to change. When we became a technology-driven society, we added stress to our lives. Now, every day, we may have hundreds of emails to answer, along with beepers that go off in the middle of the night and all day too, and urgent voice-mail messages to respond to right away. When I teach meditation, doctors who attend the workshop tell me that one of the two beepers they carry must always stay on. The other beeper can be turned off for the 20-minute meditation class.

But life isn't about rushing through it. We have to relax some of the time; relaxation adds quality to our lives. Relaxing by practicing meditation helps keep us balanced. When we feel balanced, we have a better chance of remaining healthy, and building in quality time to think about our values and goals.

What would you like to do right now that you're not doing? What hobbies have you forgotten about that you'd like to begin doing again? What enjoyable activities used to be valued and prioritized but have been long ago left behind?

We become happier when we prioritize what we value. If we value our health, for example, but don't exercise or shop for healthy food, we won't feel satisfied. It sounds simple, but prioritizing your values will make a difference in the way that you feel about yourself. In today's mad rush to get everything done, prioritizing fun activities has been relegated to last place. Everything and everybody else comes first. Women run around all day never finishing all of the items on the to-do list—and most to-do lists are too long anyway. In a "Goal Setting" workshop I facilitated, one woman described her to-do list as having babies. It's difficult to finish all of the items on your list and prioritize yourself if you don't write yourself down on that list.

To learn to prioritize yourself, begin by revising your to-do list. Only write six or seven things on a to-do list. Keep it short with your name and down time at the top. Then list the six most important activities that must be accomplished that day. Add more items only after you've finished the first six.

A to-do list that's too long is overwhelming. When we look at it, we feel stressed by all of the things we need to do and the little time that we have to do them. Before you go to bed at night, write a short list. In the morning you will wake-up with a clear mind. When you finish the six things on the list you can add more things, but don't cross out the walk that you promised yourself you were going to take at noon today.

You'll always have interruptions that slow you down, and it's tempting to take yourself off the list, but that would be a huge mistake. You are important! You are learning to prioritize yourself. Give yourself permission to come first and learn to say no. Saying no helps to control distractions.

Believe it or not, you can politely say "no" to your boss, too. Just remember to say two positive statements and then a refusal statement. For example, you can say, "The new project you're proposing sounds interesting and I like working on the team, but tonight I just can't stay late. It's family night, and I promised my children I'd take them out for dinner." (And with a boss you might want to add, "Can I begin the project tomorrow morning?")

Don't always open your scheduler every time someone asks you for a favor including the children. When someone asks you to do something for him or her, think seriously about whether or not you have the time. If you've written your personal down time into your scheduler, don't just cancel it because someone needs you to do something else. When we confuse our priorities, we add more stress to our lives, and we now know what unhealthy stress can do to our bodies and minds.

During a workshop on "Balancing Home and Work Life," a woman told me that it was important for her to begin making her lunch and carrying it with her to work. She said that she had tried to do this many times but had failed miserably. "It sounds like a simple thing," she said, "but I really want to carry my lunch to work and I just cannot get it together to do it." The woman valued her health and wanted to make a change in her diet.

When we know we want to change something, we must divide the task that we want to do into small parts. I told the woman that she had to find a specific time to shop for food each week so she'd have the ingredients she needed right at hand. This was a revelation to her. I also told her that she had to write down her goal in her scheduler and then act on it.

A goal without action steps will never be accomplished. And it is important to write things down. It helps you make a stronger commitment to the goal. It sounds simple, but when we're changing a habit like learning to put ourselves first and then taking action, the small baby steps along the way add up to success. If we make our goal and steps too large, we may fail because we get overwhelmed. Breaking down action steps into small steps and then writing the steps down helps us stick to and achieve our goals.

When I was a Weight Watchers teacher, people came to class with high expectations of how much weight they were going to lose in a month. "I will lose twenty pounds this month," women said—an unrealistic goal. When changing a habit like learning to lose weight, building meditation into our lives, or learning to prioritize ourselves in some way, we have to begin with small steps.

Here's an example from my life, something that happened several years ago. I was working a 9-to-5 job and wanted to start my own business, but I didn't know how to go about it. Should I make business cards, build a web site, print brochures? What did I need to do first? Then, one day, preparing for a workshop I began asking myself an important question. What do I value? What are my goals? I got very honest with myself.

Being honest with oneself sounds easy, but it does take practice. Everyday we spin our wheels and don't take time to find out what we think or what we feel. When I finally asked myself honest questions about the work I was doing and reviewed what I liked the most about my current job, I discovered that what I liked was the freedom the job offered. Still, I wanted to work for myself. So I began the change to full-time self-employment. It took three years. Often it was frustrating, but slowly I saw that I was making progress. Now

I make my own schedule. Because I determined what I valued, my freedom, I made a plan and pursued it, and it worked.

In my workshops, women often tell me they don't have any goals except to go to work and come home and take care of the family. One woman said, "Why rock the boat? I stopped dreaming a long time ago. Besides there isn't any time to dream. There are too many things to do."

But we have to dream. It helps us to prioritize, and when we prioritize and write our priorities on the to-do list, we're closer to keeping our commitment to ourselves. Perhaps you have heard the expression, "Life is not a dress rehearsal." The time to prioritize yourself is now!

Tips to Prioritizing Yourself

Exercise: #1

1. Ask yourself what you truly value. What is missing in your life? For example, you value being healthy.
2. Set a goal.
3. Write down specific steps to achieving the goal. For example: "I am exercising every week."
   - ❥ I will begin to walk at lunch this week for 15 minutes. I will increase that time to one-half hour twice a week by the first of the following month. By June 1st, I will reach my goal of walking three times a week for 30-40 minutes.
   - ❥ I will explore gyms in my neighborhood.
   - ❥ I will ask a friend to be a walking partner.
   - ❥ I will explore the benefits of walking and other exercise programs.

Example # 2:

If you want to begin meditating or doing any stress management program start by writing that desire down as a goal. Write it down in the present tense, as if you're already doing it. Say, for example, "I am meditating everyday." If you want to begin an exercise program, set a realistic goal of once or twice a week for 10 minutes. It's more important to do something consistently for a short time than to have an occasional spurt of energy and then drop the activity.

Every day, write an important personal goal at the top of your to-do list and then act on it. If what you're doing is not in line with what you really want and value for yourself, then shift your priorities. For example, you may want to clean out the hall closet and organize the house, but it's more important to take the children for a walk to the park. Shift the activity and take the children for a walk—or visit your parents, or exercise, play golf, write, read, garden. Be willing to shift your priorities so that the focus is on a priority personnel goal that you value.

Don't talk yourself out of the activity with negative self-talk like, "What's 10 minutes of relaxation, or exercising, or playing with the children going to do?" Remember that you're building a new habit, and that does indeed take intention, time, and a willingness to believe that you're important enough to put yourself first. It's not selfish—it's practical. I call it practical spirituality. When I take care of myself first, I have more energy and more desire to take care of all of the other pressing details and demands in my life.

Chapter 9

Feelings Make Us Visible

After 30 years as a psychotherapist, I'm still surprised at how many people, who come into therapy looking for a place to express themselves without judgment, resist accepting their own feelings and judge themselves harshly. They minimize, or suppress, or ignore their own feelings. In therapy, I help people uncover and discover rich emotional information.

Generally we're embarrassed by our emotions, especially feelings of anger, fear, shame, or jealousy. Denying our feelings not only increases our stress but makes us invisible to ourselves and to others.

In *The First Three Years of Life*, Burton White stresses the importance of negative feelings in the development of emotional stability. "At three, the child's vocabulary includes the phrase I hate you, usually said in frank honesty and quickly replaced by other emotions. Such honesty is too often intolerable to parents, however, and children quickly learn to deny or repress their own feelings. You don't really feel that way, they may be told. Only bad children hate their mommies."

"Negativism is a sign of a developing sense of self," White says. "That you have a choice, that you can say no and act in defiance of rules, is a powerful discovery to a child. A sense of mastery, of control, is awakened. However at extremes, assertions are physically crushed often accompanied by coldness or rejection."

It's no wonder that we learn to turn our backs on our emotions. Emotional development is a learned process, and the best learning comes from being allowed emotional expression and receiving validation.

The way that we feel, our emotional expression, is a part of our identity. How we express ourselves is who we are in the world. We're not just rational beings with emotions that sometimes dominate our lives. We're both rational and emotional beings, and our emotions tell us that we're alive and that we exist. Our feelings and emotions are our core energy and they need expression.

When I go into businesses to facilitate workshops, people who are desperately seeking someone to privately express their feelings to tell me how they feel, and how angry they are that no one at work is listening to them.

Unfortunately, women today have quickly learned that emotional expression has no place at work. Work environments are controlled and women suppress their emotions because any display of emotions at work is frowned upon. But suppressing emotions is like throwing away the rich kernel of the wheat germ that is filled with nourishing vitamins and nutrients. When we don't acknowledge the many ways we feel, we toss away the precious life force that gives us access to our intuition.

In the past, we believed that intellectual intelligence was the ingredient for success. But current research shows that it's how an individual manages emotional reactions that makes a difference in his or her life and career.

"Today we are being judged by a new yardstick: not just how smart we are, or by our training and expertise, but also by how well we handle ourselves and each other," Daniel Goldman says in *Emotional Intelligence*.

However, in my experience, instead of understanding emotions, people want to get rid of them. It's as if we don't have time to feel, or that it's a luxury to feel our own feelings. That's partly why antidepressants are so popular. Emotions get in the way of what we want or need to accomplish. So we brush our feelings aside and then come into therapy wondering why we're so anxious and depressed looking for a quick way to fix our feelings..

In *Looking for Spinoza: Joy, Sorrow, and the Feeling Brain* (Harcourt, 2003), Dr. Antonio Damasio, head of neurology at the University of Iowa Medical Center in Iowa City, says he's discovered "the critical role of emotions in ensuring our survival and allowing us to think. Feeling, it turns out, is not the enemy of reason, but, as Spinoza saw it, an indispensable accomplice." In other words, emotions are central to our survival. In my opinion, the best way to handle feelings is to acknowledge them—that they're normal and that you're feeling them. Ignoring emotions won't make them go away. It just leads to more problems.

Don't ignore what you feel. If you can identify your emotions, you can do something about changing your perceptions. It helps to have someone else validate your feelings too, but don't expect that to happen at work.

I like to practice one of the habits listed in Stephen Covey's book, *The Seven Habits of Highly Effective People*: "Seek to understand." When I do this, I feel that I'm in control of myself. I'm looking at a situation from another person's point of view. I keep in mind that other people have their opinions and that they're entitled to them. My opportunity is to try and understand their point of view. Doing so can de-escalate a situation, reduce stress and help adjust my perception. At the same time, I don't ignore my own feelings. I'm merely trying to understand another point of view, and at the right time, with the right person, I will express my feelings to someone, too.

When I listen to my feelings, I know the direction that I need to take. When I ignore my feelings, I create more problems for myself—just as I did when I was hospitalized. Here is a story about how listening to my feelings and following my intuition helped me to find a new home.

It was a warm September day when I drove across the Trevor Street Bridge and into the red brick apartment buildings. When I reached the dead end, I heard an inner voice, the voice of my intuition say to me, "Turn left."

"Dramatic," I said to myself, but I did as the voice said and drove around a curve and down a hill. At the next street I heard the voice inside of me say again, "Turn left again."

For six months I had been scanning the Sunday paper looking for my ideal home, close to the city but nestled in the woods, where squirrels, rabbits and deer would roam in the backyard.

For months, I met with Realtors and visited houses on streets that were built on what was once sacred Indian land. Touring these old stone homes surrounded by Japanese maples, oaks and mulberry trees, I wondered why I bothered taking up the Realtor's time. I couldn't afford to live in homes on these expensive streets. But that day I listened to the Voice of my intuition, and drove where the Voice directed. There was a For Sale sign on a house similar to the one I wanted to buy. I jotted down the Realtor's telephone number. The next day I phoned.

"Sorry," she said, "But that house was just sold."

"How much did it sell for?" I asked.

"One hundred and fifty thousand dollars," she said.

"One hundred and fifty thousand dollars?" I repeated. "I could never afford that. Could you take my telephone number in case something in my price range becomes available?"

A few days later, the Realtor phoned. The house I had inquired about was on the market again. The people who had previously signed the agreement had now backed out. That night before I went to sleep, I visualized myself standing in the dining room of that home, looking through a large plate-glass window that opened into a wooded backyard.

The next day, on a tour of my dream home, sunlight was streaming through dozens of dome-shaped skylights. As I had imagined the night before, glass windows surrounded the home. A mother deer and a baby fawn nibbled on the tall grass that grew beside Japanese maple, oak, and mulberry trees. Blue jays and robins splashed in a birdbath in the backyard.

"I can only offer the owners $125,000," I said to the Realtor. "I know it's a lot less than the asking price, but it's all I can afford."

"This is a four-bedroom, two-bath ranch on a magnificent cul-de-sac street. No house on this blocks sells for under $200,000," she said. "The one at the corner sold for over $250,000. Perhaps you should look for a home in another part of the city."

But this was my dream home.

A few days later the Realtor phoned. The owners had made a counter offer. Again I offered what I could afford. This time, the deal was signed. By listening to my feelings and following the voice of my intuition, I had found my new home.

In a workshop on "Developing Intuition," a woman told a sad story of how ignoring her intuition had led to an assault in an elevator. "I was walking home one night and looked over my shoulder to see a man following me," she said. "He followed me into my apartment building and then into the elevator. I ignored my feelings that said danger. I ignored my intuition."

The woman blamed herself for not trusting her intuition and choosing a different course of action. Women are intuitive—we've always relied on our feelings for valuable information. But in today's demanding, fast-paced world, we're losing some of this innate, instinctive ability that has guided our lives. By ignoring our intuition and our feelings, we pay a price, physically, emotionally, and spiritually.

It's time to get in touch with your feelings and intuition. Honor the richness of emotions like anger, or hurt, fear, and tiredness, too. Stop saying, "I shouldn't feel this way." Stop "shoulding" on yourself! Your feelings and your intuition are trying to tell you something. Pay attention! Don't compromise your physical, emotional, and spiritual health. Stop ignoring the fact that you need down time just for yourself. To push away feelings instead of trying to understand and deal with them is to try to hold a big beach ball under water. You can only do that for so long before it bounces up to the surface and knocks you off balance.

Allow yourself to feel. Then apply those feelings by asking yourself what's happening in your life, at home, at school, at work. What's affecting the way you feel? What are you worried about? When you get an honest sense of what's going on, you can start to solve the problem. But keep in mind that sometimes you can't always do it alone. You may need professional help—someone to help you sort out what's wrong.

From my personal experience of being hospitalized for three weeks, I've come to understand why we ignore symptoms of physical or emotional pain and thus miss out on valuable information that can help us learn about ourselves.

We've all had the experience of ignoring our emotions and saying things like "If only I'd trusted the way I felt, I wouldn't have made that mistake." It isn't uncommon to ignore what's going on inside of us. But if we remain in denial, things can get worse.

From a very young age, most of us were told that it's better to sweep feelings under the rug and be finished with them as quickly as possible. Feelings are uncomfortable, unacceptable, and messy. Throughout our lives we've heard messages like, "You don't look pretty when you cry." "Big girls don't cry." In fact, research shows that when we cry, we release chemicals into our bodies that aren't there at other times. This is one reason why people say they feel better after a good cry.

Feelings bring us messages. Sometimes the message is clear; other times it's confusing. Because we identify with our feelings, it's important to listen to them and try to sort out the message, the whisper or shout of our inner voice. Our feelings tell us we're alive. They are a guide to what's happening in our lives; they give us clues about who we are and what we may need to change. The expression of feelings makes us feel alive!

To get in touch with your feelings, increase your feeling vocabulary. Generally speaking, people's feeling vocabulary is limited to fewer than ten words. We know when we feel happy or angry, and sometimes sad. But there are hundreds of feelings. It helps to widen our feeling vocabulary. Feelings help us gauge our stress levels and may help avert crisis. Here's a "feeling" list to help you identify a wider feeling vocabulary.

Feelings Vocabulary
abandoned
annoyed
bad

betrayed
bored
burdened
calm
capable
challenged
cheated
cheerful
clever
competitive
contented
cruel
crushed
deceitful
delighted
despairing
destructive
determined
empathetic
energetic
envious
exasperated
excited
exhausted
frantic
flustered
foolish
glad
gloomy
helpless
hateful
horrible
hurt
hysterical
ignored

isolated
jealous
kind
lazy
left out
lonely
loving
lustful
mad
mean
needy
nervous
obsessed
outraged
panicked
petrified
pressured
proud
refreshed
rejected
relaxed
remorseful
scared
shocked
shy
silly
sorry
stingy
strange
stunned
stupid
talkative
tense
terrified
tired

trapped
unsettled
uneasy
wonderful
worried

Can you think of other feelings to add to the list? Doing so expands another valuable resource for your intuition, an inner guide that talks to you in your waking life as well as at night when you dream. Nourish this ability and pay attention to your nightly dreams too. As Dr. Bernie Siegel says, "Dreams are the language of the soul."

Exercise:
List 10 more feelings that are not on the above list.

Tips for increasing emotional understanding
1. Don't deny your emotions. Work to identify them. If you don't, you won't be able to work through them.
2. Close your eyes and imagine situations where you become emotional. Don't minimize what you see and feel; just experience it.
3. Practice deep breathing, feel your feelings in your belly, and allow yourself to relax.
4. In your mind's eye, embrace yourself. Embrace your emotion. I do this by wrapping my arms around myself and giving myself a hug.
5. Talk to yourself and expect an answer. Become aware of the way you think and feel.
6. Journal your feelings to deepen your relationship with yourself.

Chapter 10

Thinking Styles

In *Peace, Love, and Healing*, Dr. Bernie Seigel writes about the relationship between the state of a person's consciousness and the health of the immune system.

"Start behaving and acting as if you are the person you want to be and you will develop a sense of rhythm and harmony in your life when you are doing what feels right for you," Seigel says.

"I received similar advice a long time ago from my friend, anthropologist Ashley Montagu," Seigel adds. "When I asked him how I could become a more loving human being, he simply said, 'Behave as if you are a more loving human being.'"

Negative thinking is a habit just as positive thinking is a habit. (A habit is any practice repeated so frequently that it becomes almost automatic.) Positive self-statements indicate that you are thinking about positive aspects of a situ-

ation that can improve your stamina and increase your over-
all health. Positive thinking is a habit you can develop.

Whenever I begin a new seminar, I remind myself of my
past achievements. I say things like "I love my work. I love
teaching people positive strategies for wellness. I'm having
fun, which is important to me. I'm a competent person."

Keep in mind this important statement by Ralph Waldo
Emerson: "What you think is what you create." That means
that the way you think can affect your life and it can affect
your health.

When I was sick, I collapsed into negative self-statements
that didn't help me get well. But when I began to change the
way I was thinking, accepting my emotions and visualizing
myself as a well person again, I began to find the strength
and energy I needed to get out of bed and begin healing. Also,
I wrote down everything I was feeling, read the positive self-
statements aloud, and ended on a note of self-approval. I was
developing the thinking style of positive thinking.

The way we think either adds to stress or diminishes it.
Here are some examples of faulty thinking styles from *Psy-
chology of Adjustment, An Applied Approach* by Thomas
Creer. Which ones do you use?

Thinking Styles

1. **Magnification**. You magnify negative details while
   filtering out positive aspects of a situation.
2. **Polarized Thinking**. Things are either black or white,
   good or bad. There is no middle ground.
3. **Overgeneralization**. You tend to make broad
   conclusions based on a little data. If something bad
   happens to you, you expect its reoccurrence again
   and again.
4. **Mind Reading**. You believe you know what other
   people are thinking or feeling toward you without their
   saying anything.

5. **Catastrophizing**. You make a catastrophe out of events. You come to expect disaster and to think in "what ifs."

6. **Personalization**. This is related to mind reading in that you believe everything a person does is somehow related to your behavior. You compare yourself to others in terms of who is smarter, better looking, etc.

7. **Control Fallacies**. This one has two parts: (A) If you think you have little control over an event, you see yourself as totally helpless. Your future is at the whim of someone or something else. (B) If you believe you have some control over an event, you somehow feel you're responsible for any unhappiness experienced by others. If they experience failure you feel it's your fault.

8. **Fallacy of Fairness**. You're resentful because you're certain you know what's fair, even when others disagree with you. You may hold on to the idea that life is fair, although there's no evidence that this is the case.

9. **Blaming**. You hold others responsible for whatever problems you experience.

10. **"Shoulding."** You have rules about how you think you and others should act. When others do not behave the way you think they should, you become angry. When you don't act the way you think you should, you feel guilt or shame.

11. **Emotional Reasoning**. You let your emotions dictate your "should beliefs."—If you feel dumb, you must be dumb. You don't consider the fact that emotions don't obey any laws of reason.

Creer, T.L., *Psychology of Adjustment,* 1977, pp. 76-77. Reprinted by permission of Pearson Education Inc., Upper Saddle River, NJ.

12. **Fallacy of Change**. You feel you can change people if you try hard enough. If you do change them, you think it will increase your happiness.
13. **Global Labeling**. You generalize one or two qualities into a global judgment. For instance, if you perform poorly at one or two tasks, you decide you must be stupid and incapable of performing any task well.
14. **Being Right**. You feel you must be continually on trial to prove your behaviors and opinions are correct. Being wrong is unthinkable; you will go to any length to demonstrate that you are right.
15. **Heaven's Reward Fallacy**. You expect all your actions to pay off as if someone is keeping score. You feel bitter when what you perceive as your just reward doesn't happen. At the same time, you feel angry when someone receives what you perceive as a reward they do not deserve.
16. **Vengeance**. You have thoughts of getting back at another person or harming them in some way.
17. **Labeling**. You tend to categorize people negatively as stupid, a jerk, dumb, inconsiderate.

One of my favorite stories that illustrates different thinking styles happened in my own family when my son was nine years old. He wanted to learn to ski, so we drove to the mountains and by the time I had my ski boots fastened, he was already on the slopes and skiing downhill. I was sliding across the snow, struggling to keep my balance, when I looked up to see him racing toward me. Immediately I begin an inner dialogue, rehearsing what I planned to say to him. A few seconds later he glided to a neat stop in front of me

"Where are your ski poles?" I demanded.

"I don't need them," he boasted. "I can ski without them. I'm a good athlete—it's easy! Anybody can do it!"

At nine years old, my son didn't have the same limiting beliefs about his athletic abilities that I had about mine. Skiing was easy for him. He also didn't have the same memories I had of once warming the bench on the hockey field and later being laughed at in the locker room for running down the field in the wrong direction. Still, I insisted that he accompany me to a ski lesson. While I hung on to my ski poles, he made angels in the snow. When the class ended, he went up the hill and down again without poles.

Another anecdote emphasizing this point concerns two monks who took vows of chastity and silence. As they were walking, they met a woman who needed help crossing a river. Seeing her problem, one monk lifted her and carried her to the other side. Then the two monks continued their walk. When they stopped for the evening meal and the silence could be broken, the second monk said, "This morning when you carried the woman across the river, you broke your vow of chastity." The first monk replied, "Dear friend, I put the young woman down this morning, but you've been carrying her ever since." It's the same with the way we think and the beliefs we carry around with us. They're often self-defeating and negative and difficult to let go of.

People have different thinking styles at different times. You might be someone who magnifies events, focuses on the negative, and filters out the positive. Others are rigid about observing rules. Some express strong opinions about what others should or shouldn't do. And many people need to prove that they're right all the time. Some expect the worst to happen and are overly concerned with failure.

If you focus only on the negatives of a situation, chances are that your inner dialogue will be negative and your life will feel out of balance. Meditation helps a person to feel balance and can assist with creating a more harmonious consciousness so that it is easier to change faulty thinking styles or, as Bernie Seigel says, "Act as if."

Chapter 11

Visualizations and Affirmations

Visualization or "imagined rehearsal," Thomas Creer says in *Psychology of Adjustment, An Applied Approach*, "entails rehearsing behavior in your imagination. There is evidence that this approach can be effective particularly in improving motor skills" in sports like swimming or running or any activity involved in improving athletic performance.

Here are the nine steps he outlines for using Imagined Rehearsal effectively:

1. Rehearse coping skills that you use in real life.
2. Actively imagine the situation as clearly as possible.
3. Imagine the situation and your behavior in complete, minute detail.
4. Rehearse your performance in the actual setting, if possible.
5. Practice any rehearsed activity in its entirety.
6. Imagined rehearsal should be successful.

7. At least one mental practice should precede actual physical performance.
8. Rehearsal should proceed at the same speed at which behavior unfolds in real life.
9. In rehearsal, concentrate on imagining the feel of a situation.

When I was hospitalized for colitis, I began using visualization and affirmations—positive self-statements to help me change the image of myself. I made a decision to see myself as a strong and healthy woman. Then, every day, I visualized and said, "I have energy, I have stamina, I am strong, I am in control of my life." As I said these affirmations, positive self-statements dozens of times a day, in a very real sense I was giving myself pep talks. When a negative thought entered my mind I pushed it away and I replaced it with a positive self-statement and a positive visualization.

When I was hospitalized I lived with depression, anxiety, and fear, and worried about what was not happening in my life. At the same time that I was worrying, I was becoming accustomed to these feelings. I knew that having colitis was not a healthy state, yet I chose to ignore the symptoms, hoping I could heal myself naturally. Instead, I found I no longer believed in myself and worry replaced my ability to practice visualization and affirmations. I now know that depression and anxiety affect health and emotions. Prior to my hospitalization, the anxiety and extra stress that I'd ignored took a toll on my immune system. I was restless, nervous, and withdrawn, irritable during the day and sleeping poorly at night. I lived with this response instead of confronting the situation and sharing the heartache that I felt.

When stress becomes long-term and there's no relief or any way to successfully manage it, it hurts us physically.

Creer, T.L., *Psychology of Adjustment,* 1977, pp. 69. Reprinted by permission of Pearson Education Inc., Upper Saddle River, NJ.

Researchers say cumulative stress isn't limited to major events, but can also be produced by minor daily hassles.

Stress is impossible to avoid, but you don't have to become its victim. The key is to acknowledge what's going on in your life and then decide to act on the stresses by changing your response to them.

For example, on your drive home from work tonight, begin to become conscious of your breathing. As we now know, Conscious Breathing helps you to relax. It also gets you ready for your next activity.

Decide how you want to act when you come into your house. Make a conscious decision about how you're going to greet your family. Visualize the love you have for them before you step in the door. Begin your evening with these affirmations.

Affirmations

1. I am the author of my experiences, attitudes, and actions, and not the victim of fate or circumstance.
2. I am a loving person.
3. My heart is filled with grace and love.
4. I bless my present job with love, knowing it is a stepping stone on my journey.
5. My work is fulfilling and joyous, and a natural expression of my creativity.
6. I cherish my family, my children, and my spouse.
7. My body is dancing with joy and happiness.
8. I listen to my inner voice and the wisdom of my body and mind.
9. I will enter the house with a relaxed state of mind, suspending my judgments of what needs to or should have been done.
10. I let go of what I cannot control.

11. Forgiveness opens my mind and heart to new ways of seeing others. It frees me from my past. I bless all my past relationships and the people in them.
12. Adversity is a stepping stone to my success.
13. Every day I bless all of the people in my life.
14. I am looking towards the future, knowing that God is guiding my every action and that there is a Divine Plan for my life.
15. New opportunities abound. I am lucky. I am blessed.
16. I am a good friend. I care about other people. Others care about me.
17. I am patient, especially with the people in my life I love the most.
18. I take care of myself. I tell people when I need five minutes of time just for me.
19. Every person that I meet has something to teach me.
20. I have a passion for learning and for teaching.
21. I am a positive thinker.
22. I am relaxing.
23. I give myself permission to make time for myself.

I love to make up affirmations and I say them every day. I anchor them to specific times, like the drive to and from my office. I also say affirmations when I'm in the shower or before I fall asleep at night. Before bed, I have a ritual of mentally scanning my body and blessing myself. I ask my body if there is any message that it needs to tell me. Is there something that I need to do? Sometimes I get an answer like, "You are forgetting to drink water. You are not exercising as much as you used to." Then the next day I make time to do that. I honor the message to take care of myself.

Visualizing means intentionally forming mental pictures. It works because it gives us the feeling of controlling a situation. Visualization inspires and makes us hopeful that a good outcome is possible.

Creer notes that visualization acts as a "stress inocula-
tion." We lessen problems by preparing for them. Visualization is a coping strategy, too. "Remember," Creer says,
"the more you rehearse and practice your coping strategy,
the more successful you are likely to be in your life."

I like to think of visualization as productive daydream-
ing. It's not a way to escape from the real world, but a creative way to cope with problems and help shape positive
outcomes in our lives. Thousands of people use visualization to activate their imaginations every day, to reduce stress
and tension, to learn to get control of their lives and health.
Positive visualizations boost self-esteem and change your
state of mind.

Not everyone visualizes or forms mental pictures in the
same way. You can visualize from thoughts in the present,
from memories, or a past positive experience. You can imagine something you want to happen in the future. If you find
it difficult to visualize, take an image from a good movie or
book that makes you feel happy, and then use that image
to visualize yourself. Put yourself in the place of the char-
acter you admired or who made you laugh. Positive images
of strength, success, and relaxation make you feel you are
in charge of your life.

When I'm tense, I simply see myself sitting in my favorite
lounge chair. I close my eyes and wrap myself in a warm
mental blanket. I feel relaxed. Visualization is that simple,
and it works.

Athletes use visualization to practice winning games.
One research study matched two groups of athletes. The
first group practiced actually swimming in a pool. The second group visualized swimming and winning, but never actually went into the pool. In the competition that followed, both
groups did equally well. The mental rehearsing of images
and outcomes in this study proved just as effective as physically practicing the sport. It is the same with just about any-

thing you want to have happen in your life and your health: It happens first in your mind.

In Vietnam, a prisoner of war visualized playing 18 holes of golf at his favorite golf course. For seven years, he visualized each shot in great detail. In his mind, he picked up the clubs, walked the course, carefully lined up each shot, assumed his stance, and then hit the ball. Each time, he saw himself scoring in the 70s, even though before he was imprisoned, his best score on that course had been 85. When he was finally released from the prison camp, he went to the course he'd been visualizing all those years and played his round of golf. His final score was in the 70s, just as he'd visualized as a POW.

Before I go into a potentially stressful meeting, I visualize myself walking on the beach. The ocean is a strong soothing image for me. I see seagulls flying overhead, and hear the gentle waves of the ocean rushing towards the shore. If I want to visualize the positive result of the meeting, I do so from this relaxed state, seeing myself positively received by the other people. It works. If you don't give your mind a goal to reach for, it will drift endlessly, often towards negativity. But you're in charge. Use visualization as a powerful, personal, positive strategy for your wellness, and to get a few minutes of relaxing down time for yourself.

Norman Cousins is a great example of the use of visualization to boost the immune system. In his book, *Head First*, he wrote, "Emotions and health are closely related. It has been known for many years that negative emotions and experiences can have a deleterious effect on health and can complicate medical treatment. Not as well-known is the connection between positive attitudes and the possible enhancement of the body's healing system."

What happens when people negatively visualize themselves is that they tell themselves they're unable to perform a task because they're clumsy or they believe they're a fail-

ure or that they will never be able to find down time for themselves. Because they visualize themselves negatively, they'll
get negative results. Visualization is a powerful tool that's
both intentional and positive.

Practice visualization exercises every night before you
drift off to sleep. These exercises should take no more then
a few minutes of your time.

Visualization:
1. Begin with Conscious Breathing, slowly inhaling and
   exhaling, putting your attention on your breath.
2. Allow an image of yourself or a feeling about yourself
   to come into your mind.
3. See yourself with a smile on your face. You are a
   lovely human being. Give yourself a hug. Have
   compassion and love for yourself first.
4. Finish the visualization with, "I am letting go. I am
   releasing the tensions of the day. I love and accept
   myself just the way I am. I am grateful for who I am."

No matter what your thinking style, affirmations and visualizations reduce the stress of any situation. It is a simple
way to relax and get a few minutes of down time for yourself.

Chapter 12

Writing Helps to Heal

When I write, words are a song in my mind. Like the sweet soothing sounds of the robins chirping outside my window at eight o'clock in the morning, words sing to me. They dance on the page and create images in my mind. Sometimes the images are strong. When they are weak I search for the right way to express something that I am feeling. While I search I continue to write, even if what I'm writing isn't exactly what I want to say. Writing is one of my favorite ways to get down time for myself. It is private, personal, and rewarding.

Words have a sound. Some people call it a writer's voice. To make writing simple, write the way that you talk. Don't judge what you write. Editing comes later. Weave in the senses: touch, taste, feel, smell, and hearing. Writing helps to relieve stress, and it's easy to do.

Write for five minutes a day in a notebook or a journal. Hold the critic back, the part of the self that wants to check the grammar, spelling, and edit the page you just wrote. Write down your thoughts and feelings. Keep writing and see where it takes you. Sometimes writing helps to clarify values and priorities. Let the words flow. Don't worry about what you're saying. Just say it and be honest. Write for yourself.

Make a date with yourself to write. You are making a commitment to yourself. When you sit down to write, you may still feel resistance. That stuck feeling may be saying that there is something to think about. I work with the stuck feeling by talking to myself. I ask, "Tell me how you're feeling today, Ruth." When I start to write, I don't always feel good. When I finish, I usually feel happy and relaxed. I cherish my writing time and I try to do it first thing in the morning before the activities of the day begin.

Quick, Fun Writing Exercises

Exercise #1

Begin with Conscious Breathing, centering yourself. Put your hand on your belly. Pay attention to your feelings in your solar plexus area. Now see if you can identify a color in your mind. Describe this color. Is it yellow? Does it remind you of sunshine? Is it being on the beach, or perhaps staring out the window and wanting to go outside and play at recess? Write about it. If the color is blue, does it remind you of the ocean? Write about it.

Exercise #2

Feeling rejected is fairly common in life. Often, when we feel rejected, we feel it in our solar plexus. Close your eyes and put your hand on your belly. Think about a time that you felt rejected. What did you learn from it? How did this incident impact the way that you see yourself today? Begin to write about that incident.

Exercise #3

Close your eyes and visualize yourself as a child. What did you look like? How did you act? Were you shy, timid, bold, or outrageous? What did you think about? How did you feel? What did you like to do? Who did you play with? Who were you close to? Did you have a best friend? Questions like these can help you think back and reflect. Write about yourself.

Exercise #4

Pick a scene from your childhood. For example, you're playing in the backyard, or you're in your bedroom. Perhaps it's a scene at the dinner table or in the school-yard. What was happening in that scene? What were you thinking? How did you feel? What did you look like? Describe in as much detail as you can.

Exercise #5

Do you remember your first significant love? Who was this person? What happened? Did you spend time together or was it a fantasy? Describe your first love.

Exercise #6

Do you remember your first day at school? Close your eyes and think back. Write from the feeling level. You may not remember the details, but you can remember the emotions. Write from that place.

Exercise #7

Where were you born? Did you grow up in the same city you were born in? How did your parents choose your name? Was your name ever shortened to a nick-name? When you were called by the shortened version, did it have a meaning? Write about that meaning.

My mother nicknamed me Rudy, and was the only person who called me by that name. When she did, I knew she was happy with me. I felt her love. Before leaving the house in the morning she would say, "Ready Rudy?" I replied, "Rudy ready." That's one of the warmest and fondest memories I have of my mother and me.

Exercise #8

As a child, what did you look like? Describe your face, eyes, nose, mouth, hair, and ears. Did you have any distinguishing marks that made you feel a certain way? Were you outgoing or shy? How did you feel inside? How was that different from the way you think others perceived you?

Exercise #9

Describe your home or, if you lived in several differ-ent homes, pick one to write about. What do you remember most about your home? What was your bed-room like? Did you share a room? Did you have your own bed? If you shared with someone, who was it? What was it like sleeping with that person? How did you feel? What did you think? Do you remember the tex-tures in your room? Wool? Cottons? Lace? What col-ors do you recall?

Exercise #10

Growing up, who were you close to? What did they look like? How did they talk to you? Did they have a smell you recall? Did you live with this person? What do you remember the most about this person?

Exercise #11

Make a list of the turning points in your life. Let the list grow. Pick one turning point and write about it. During this time did you move? Were you happy with the change? Did it bring you satisfaction? Write about a turning point that brought you the most pain. How did your views about life change?

Exercise #12

We all have regrets. "I should have, could have, would have. If only I had." We qualify our regrets and we minimize them. Write about one of your regrets that still makes your heart ache. Use as many feeling words as you can to describe the regret. Write for 10 minutes. Some examples of feelings are- feeling blamed, guilt, unfairness, lack of respect, frustration, shame, embarrassment, feeling left out.

Exercise #13

Close your eyes. Recall a provocation. Think about the details. Write them down. Share the writing with someone you trust. Ask them to be a good listener and not to judge you.

Honest writing means just that. When you write, be honest with yourself. Write the way you feel about an event. Honest writing touches hearts. And it's an easy and effective tool for reducing stress and a fun way to use down time. Jotting down our thoughts even while at work creates some psychological space from the activity around us. Briefly, it allows us to focus on ourselves and creates private time—a few minutes at work just for you.

Chapter 13

Good Communication Reduces Stress

Good communication reduces stress. When we're good communicators, we actually increase our efficiency, which results in more personal time for ourselves. When we communicate poorly we end up having to sort out the problems we created. This takes time away from our down time.

Good communication is intentional, focused and conscious. We pay attention to what we want to say. A good communication is planned and delivers a focused message. During the communication, we absolutely avoid interrupting other people, preaching, philosophizing, or blaming others, just to name a few of the roadblocks to good communication.

Keep in mind that hearing and listening are different. Hearing is involuntary; listening is voluntary and selective.

We have to choose to listen, and we do tune out. Generally, we listen when a conversation is interesting to us. Or we listen to what someone is saying because we feel like listening, or perhaps we listen because we feel we might miss something. Being a good listener is a learned skill. Check the following and see if you qualify.

Good-Listener Checklist
1. Do you daydream while others are talking?
2. Do you often interrupt while others are talking?
3. Do you feel an urgency inside of you that makes you want to tell your opinion when someone is talking?
4. When someone is talking, are you thinking about what you are going to say next?
5. Do you find that you often finish sentences for people when they are talking?
6. When someone is talking to you, do you continue working on the computer or opening mail?

How many of those did you say "yes" to? More than two yes answers means you need to tune up your listening skills.

When I'm in a therapy session with someone, I tune in to him or her and listen closely to what that person is saying. I'm also aware of the way I feel. Is my body comfortable? Am I tired? Am I fully present? Maybe I have something on my mind. Because I'm trained to listen, I can relax and tune into the other person. You can learn that, too. As a good listener, you focus 100 percent of your attention on the speaker. Anything less than that diminishes communication. It's impossible to have a good communication with someone who's watching television, surfing the Internet, or glancing at a watch. Distraction creates frustration, which you can avoid by asking what would be a good time to get undivided attention.

Effective communication techniques do reduce stress. If you're familiar with the classic "I" statements, then you know that when you use the word "I" and talk about your feelings, it clarifies for the other person what you think and feel. It also has the effect of reducing defensiveness and improving communication. The more you work on improving communication, the less time you'll spend defending or explaining yourself. As a result, you'll have more time for yourself to do the things that you really want to do just for you.

"I" statements force you to take responsibility for your feelings. Others don't feel blamed when we take responsibility for our part of a communication. When we use the word "you," we point a finger that can make another person feel blamed, criticized, or attacked. Here's an example: Spouse says, "You are always criticizing me." Instead, spouse says: "I feel upset when you say that. I feel that you are blaming me."

An On-the-Job Example

Sender: "The problem with the missing pages from the report has been identified and is being worked on. I don't need to discuss it anymore."

Receiver: "I want to be clear about what you are saying. You are saying that you don't want to discuss the problem about the missing pages from the report. The problems are being worked on, and perhaps the team will be getting together at the end of the week to discuss the project. Is that right?"

The receiver is paraphrasing and asking an open-ended question. Open-ended questions include what, when, where, why. They elicit conversation and cool down emotional discussions, letting the other person know that you are interested in what he or she is saying.

When a person is speaking, choose to remain silent. The longer you do so, the more information you'll get, and the better understanding you'll have about the other person and about the topic. It's my experience that people keep on talking and talking to make their point. If I make a conscious choice to remain silent, and begin Conscious Breathing to balance and center myself, I have more control of my end of the conversation. I'm also using my time well. Instead of standing in front of the person feeling tense and irritated. I am relaxing and breathing.

I am using nonverbal cues. Nodding my head and saying, "ah," or "uh-huh," or "umm," "I see," "okay," or "I understand," at the right places communicates caring and interest. Nonverbal communication encourages the other person, as do positive facial expressions.

When the other person finishes speaking, paraphrase or restate what he or she said. Paraphrasing is a mirroring technique that helps clarify what the other person has said. It's especially useful when the conversation is emotional or contains a lot of detail. To help clarify a conversation you can say. "I want to understand exactly what you're telling me." Then in your words, using many of the same words that the other person used, paraphrase what he or she said. For example your spouse may say, "I can't take it when you leave wet towels on the bed." You might then paraphrase or mirror, and say "So what you're saying is that it upsets you when I leave wet towels on the bed."

Paraphrasing lets the other person know that you're listening. Pay attention to your facial expressions and your tone of voice. Body language is important, too. If you look away or fold your arms across your chest, that takes energy from the conversation. Paraphrasing communicates interest and understanding.

Open-ended questions ask, what, when, where, and why. Closed-ended questions have different responses. Closed-ended questions require only a yes or no response. Both are useful; it's just a matter of using what you need to increase effective communication.

Here's a checklist:
1. Use silence.
2. Be aware of your body language, facial expression, and nonverbal cues.
3. Ask open-ended questions.
4. Ask, "Is there anything more that you want to tell me about this situation?" Restate or paraphrase what was said, using words the other person used.
5. Ask, "Did I get that?"

Communication Skills Tips
1. Keep your mind on the goal of the communication. Plan your communication to reach that goal.
2. Share your thoughts and feelings.
3. Be honest and specific.
4. Accentuate the positive. Give praise.
5. Clarify what you need to have happen through open-ended questions.
6. Use "I" messages.
7. Stay calm and neutral.
8. Contain difficult emotions.
9. Listen more than you talk.
10. Be aware of body language.
11. Give the person time to respond.
12. Don't be defensive.
13. Seek agreement on the situation being discussed and what may have caused the problem.
14. Avoid finger pointing and blaming.
15. Discuss alternatives.
16. If there's only one solution, then clearly state that there's only one solution.
17. Avoid threatening, lecturing, judging, or ridiculing.
18. Deliver negative messages in private. Don't embarrass another person.

19. Don't procrastinate about giving important feedback even if it's difficult to do so.
20. Don't gossip.
21. Use a constructive, problem-solving approach.
22. Show genuine concern and respect for the other person.
23. Use active listening skills such as paraphrasing and mirroring.
24. Say what you mean in a supportive tone of voice.
25. Validate difficulties and continue on to a solution.
26. Create clear boundaries between you and the other person. Don't make their defensiveness your own.
27. See yourself as a part of a winning team that supports clear communication and allows feedback.

Active Listening
1. Relaxed, receptive body language.
2. Sender initiates a communication.
3. Receiver paraphrases using the sender's words, or directly mirrors the response.
4. Receiver can say, "If I heard you correctly," or, "Okay, I hear what you're saying. You are saying..." or "I want to make sure I understand what you are saying. You are saying..." Then mirror back or paraphrase using the words that the other person said.

Points to Keep in Mind
1. We want to get our point across.
2. We want to be heard.
3. Often we feel an urgency to be understood and heard.
4. We want to be validated. Sometimes (or often) others will miss our point and not hear the message.
5. Relationships get hurt.
6. We miss out on closeness.

7. We stay locked into old patterns.
8. Be willing to try something new.
9. Be aware that new skills take time and effort to develop.
10. There is no perfection.
11. We will make mistakes.
12. Over and over again.
13. Things will improve.
14. Only to go backwards again.
15. Pick yourself up.
16. Dust off.
17. Try again.

Chapter 14

Praying Relieves Stress

Dr. Larry Dossey, author of *Reinventing Medicine, Beyond Mind-Body to a New Era of Healing*, talks in his book about a scientific study of prayer. "Over a 10-month period researchers gathered patients who said they'd like to be prayed for, until they had 393 participants and another 201 in a control group that wasn't included in the prayers. The results were striking, even to skeptics. The patients who were prayed for were five times less likely to need antibiotics than those who had nobody praying for them. They were three times less likely to have pulmonary edema, and fewer patients died in the prayed-for group than in the control group."

Prayer works and we don't need scientific studies to tell us so. Prayer makes us feel good, and when we feel good we can do more, with a better attitude, and have time left for ourselves. In the hospital the affirmations I used were a form of prayer known as "I AM" affirmations.

In the "I AM" discourses by Godfre Ray King the phrase, "I am" is a call to the God-Presence. "The I AM Presence," King says, "brings forward what the person making the call desires, immediately turning all the energy of your being to the center in the brain, which is the source of being."

"If one would take this statement, 'I AM the Presence thinking through this mind and body,' he or she would receive some remarkable ideas," King continues. "The brain is the first point where obstruction begins to register, because it is the point of contact with wrong ideas. Wrong ideas register most quickly and intensely in the brain structure because that is the field of atomic activity." Current research supports Godfre Ray King's thinking confirming that our brain cells increase when we pray and speak words of gratitude and appreciation.

A 1996 *Time Magazine* article entitled "Faith and Healing," discussed a 1995 study at Dartmouth-Hitchcock Medical Center that had found this: "One of the best predictors of survival among 232 heart surgery patients was the degree to which the patients said they drew comfort and strength from their religious faith. Those who did not have faith had three times the death rate of those who did. Numerous studies have found lower rates of depression and anxiety-related illness among the religiously committed."

Praying is an effective and simple way to make personal time. You can be sitting at your desk, riding in your car, standing in line at the supermarket, or watching television. You can talk silently to yourself any time of day or night. Practiced with the right mental attitude and with sincerity, prayer is instantly relaxing. And prayer can release our fears and worries, especially when we wake up in the middle of the night from a frightening dream and adrenaline is pouring into our body making us feel afraid.

When we pray, we are giving thanks. We're surrendering, and we're acknowledging that there's something more powerful than our little egos. Prayer helps us to stop mentally chewing on things. Prayer helps us let go of the things over which we have no control. When we pray, we set positive energy into motion. Praying takes the burden off our shoulders and helps us relax.

After the devastation of 9-11, I was asked to go to New York and facilitate groups in companies located around Ground Zero. These companies needed a grief counselor to support their employees, most of whom had directly witnessed that terrifying nightmare. I was happy to go to New York, but I was also scared.

When I got there I took a cab to Canal Street and then walked the rest of the way to Wall Street, many blocks from Ground Zero. Along the way I showed identification to Army personnel. During the long walk I took many conscious breaths and I prayed.

"Help me to facilitate support groups and do no harm. And thank you for letting me help." Praying gave me courage. It allowed me to lean on something greater than myself.

When we get caught up in our busy lives, we often forget that a powerful force guides us and is always there ready to comfort us. Praying helps us to let go of stress and tension, events and people that we have no control over. On my walk to Ground Zero I kept repeating, "God's Will is guiding my life." It is a simple prayer, but it made me feel God was with me and that I would be okay. It helped me let go of my fears.

A favorite prayer said by millions of people every day around the world is the Great Invocation. It is a prayer of hope and a call for peace. Triangles, an organization in New York, sponsors this prayer. "The Great Invocation is a service activity for men and women of goodwill who believe in the power of thought." Visualizing connecting triangles of light the following prayer is said:

"From the point of light within the mind of God,
Let light stream forth into the minds of men.
Let light descend on earth.
From the point of love within the heart of God,
Let love stream forth into the hearts of men.
May Christ return to earth.
From the center where the will of God is known,
Let purpose guide the little wills of men,
The purpose which the masters know and serve.
From the center which we call the race of men,
Let the plan of love and light work out.
And may it seal the door where evil dwells.
Let love, light, power, and wisdom,
restore God's plan on earth."

Another powerful and popular prayer recited today in many 12-step programs is the Serenity Prayer:
"God, grant me
the Serenity to accept the things I cannot change,
the Courage to change the things I can,
and the Wisdom to know the difference."

Some other favorite prayers include these:
"Praise God from whom all blessings flow;
Praise Him, all creatures here and below;
Praise Him above, Ye Heavenly Host." (Traditional hymn, words by Thomas Ken, 1674.)

"I release all of my past, negatives, fears, human relationships, self-image, future, and human desires to the Light. I am a Light Being. I radiate the Light from my Light Center throughout my being. I radiate the Light from my Light Center to everyone. I radiate the Light from my Light Center to everything. I am in a bubble of Light and only Light can come to me and only Light can be here. Thank you God for everyone, for everything, and for me." (*Seven Steps of Effective Prayer*, by Jim Goure.)

"Our Father, who art in heaven, hallowed be Thy name. Thy kingdom come, Thy will be done on earth, as it is in heaven. Give us this day our daily bread. And forgive us our trespasses, as we forgive those who trespass against us. And lead us not into temptation, but deliver us from evil, For Thine is the kingdom, and the power, and the glory, forever and ever. Amen." ("The Lord's Prayer.")

"How wonderful, O Lord, are the works of your hands! The heavens declare Your glory, the arch of the sky displays Your handiwork. In Your love You have given us the power to behold the beauty of Your world robed in all its splendor. The sun and the stars, the valleys and the hills, the rivers and the lakes all disclose Your presence. The roaring breakers of the sea tell of Your awesome might, the beauty of the field and birds of the airs bespeak Your wondrous will. In Your goodness, You made us able to hear the music of the world. The voices of the loved ones reveal to us that You are in our midst, a divine voice sings through all creation." (Traditional Jewish prayer.)

"Shima, Yisrael, Adonai Elohanu. Adonai Echad. Hear, O Israel: The Lord our God, The Lord is One. And thou shalt love the Lord thy God with all thy heart, and with all thy soul, and with all thy might." (Bible: Deuteronomy.)

"Father, I abandon myself into Your hands; do with me what You will. Whatever You may do, I thank You: I am ready for all, I accept all. Let only Your will be done in me, and in all Your creatures. I wish no more than this, O Lord. Into Your hands, I commend my soul; I offer it to You with all the love of my heart, for I love You, Lord, and so need to give myself, to surrender myself into Your hands; without reserve, and with boundless confidence. For You are my Father. ("Prayer of Abandonment," Charles de Foucauld.)

"To everything there is a season, a time for every purpose under the sun. A time to be born and a time to die; a time to plant and time to pluck up that which is planted; a time to kill and a time to heal. A time to weep and a time to laugh; a time to mourn and a time to dance. A time to embrace and a time to refrain from embracing; a time to lose and a time to seek; a time to rend and a time to sew; a time to keep silent and a time to speak; a time to love and a time to hate; a time for war and a time for peace. (Ecclesiastes.)

Here's a short simple prayer of gratitude I wrote and say everyday:

"I love taking care of myself and having personal time just for me. My heart is filled with love and gratitude for all of Nature and for the wonderful people that I meet."

Chapter 15

100 Tips for the 100-MPH Woman

Every day, pick one of these ideas to think about. Write it down and post it on your computer or in your scheduler. Read it often during the day.

1. Learn to say "No." When you do, you will have a happier and more balanced life.
2. Let go of what you can't control. Letting go brings peace of mind.
3. Take care of yourself every day. Do something special just for you. Take a bubble bath. Read a magazine. Sit down and close your eyes for five minutes. Go for a walk.
4. Think positive thoughts. The way you think is one thing you do have control over.
5. Compliment yourself all day. Toot your own horn. Say things like, "I am doing something special just for me, guilt free. I like myself. I am happy about my life."

6. Give up needing to be perfect. Do the best you can. Forgive yourself for your mistakes.

7. Keep your expectations reasonable. Delegate, delegate, and delegate.

8. Imagine fresh, clean, clear oxygen flooding your cells and the organs of your body, relaxing you. Conscious breathing oxygenates the body. Breathing helps control and reduce stress.

9. When you get upset, count to 10. This helps buy time so that you can respond with control and not react.

10. Use "I" statements. Say, "I need time for myself." "I need a break." "Can you help?"

11. Dinner doesn't have to be perfect. Sometimes pizza is fine for dinner. On the weekends, cook and freeze several microwavable meals for rushed weekday meals.

12. Schedule weekly family meetings. Bring a timer to the meeting. Let everyone express his or her feelings for 3-5 minutes. Write down your expectations about chores etc. Post them on the refrigerator. Review them at the next meeting.

13. After work when you're tired, say to your family, "When I come home, I am going into my room and relax for 10 minutes." Take a 10-minute break before moving on to the next activity.

14. Keep a magnetized pad and paper on the refrigerator and mark down needed grocery items. Divide the shopping chores.

15. Delegate. Ask, "Can you pick up the milk?" "Can you get the dry cleaning on your way home from work?"

16. Decide what your priorities are each day and do them first.

17. Think before you say "yes" to something that someone else wants you do.

18. Monitor self-talk. Don't enrage yourself with angry thoughts. You may end up winning the battle but

losing a relationship or a good job. Try and stay open to other people's points of view. Say to yourself, "She's just expressing herself. Her point of view has to do with her, not with me. I choose not to be hurt by her point of view." Or by his.

19. Visualize the kind of day you want to have before you get out of bed. Visualize a happy day being with people that support you.

20. Practice Conscious Breathing. Meditate, exercise, visualize, read, garden, journal, play golf, etc. Anything just for you!

21. When you need a break, take a time-out for yourself. Say, "I need time to think this over. Can we talk later?" Walk away.

22. God is watching over me and guiding my life. She needs me to be a co-creator with Her to help me maximize my potential. My Higher Power is taking care of me, prospers me, and keeps me safe in all that I do.

23. Schedule time for yourself just as you would a meeting.

24. Go to workshops and seminars to keep learning and upgrading your skills.

25. Don't skip breakfast. Your body needs fuel in the morning. You won't lose weight by skipping one meal.

26. Be kind to your body. Praise it, whatever shape it's in. Every morning when you wake up say, "I love my body and I love myself. Yes I do. I love you, love you, love you!"

27. Get a massage.

28. Before going to work, put the wash in the washer. When you return home after work, throw it in the dryer.

29. Have a place for your keys and keep them there.

30. At night, get a good rest. Go to bed at a reasonable time.

31. On your morning and evening commute, listen to audio, self-help, or classical music tapes or CDs.

32. When you're stuck in traffic, open a cigar box filled with an emory board, nail clipper, hand lotion, dental floss, etc.
33. Have a basket for mail. Sort it at least once a week.
34. Prepare lunches the night before.
35. When cooking, turn on music or watch TV.
36. Divide the chores. If you find that after a hard day at work, you're the only person in the family doing most of the work at home, something is out of balance. Change it!
37. It's okay to user paper plates for meals.
38. On Sunday night, review with other family members what needs to be done for the week ahead. Divide the shopping chores. Put the jobs on a sticky pad. Hand them out.
39. Tell your children the reasons they need to help around the house. Reward them, but don't micromanage their jobs.
40. Practice meditation at least once a day for 15 minutes.
41. Is there an exercise room at work? Take advantage of it. If not, walk at lunch for 10 minutes, or when possible, exercise before you come home.
42. Have fresh carrots, raisins and other quick delicious snacks ready to hold the hungry family over until dinner is ready.
43. Ask for help before you sink into despair and anger.
44. Children need a consistent bedtime ritual. Put them to bed on time and you can have time for yourself.
45. At work, write down what you eat during the day. Writing down what you eat helps eating habits stay under control.
46. Stop dieting and eat wholesome foods.
47. Let go of the need to change your ex. He is somebody you really can't control!

48. Drink plenty of water. Carry a water bottle with you and drink.
49. Instead of fast food keep a diet shake in your car for food emergencies.
50. Say affirmations every day. They make you feel good. Say, "I love myself. I'm good enough. I am a worthwhile person. My work is valued. My children are happy. I am grateful for the wonderful things in my life. I am abundant. I prosper in everything that I do. My body is in good health. I eat nourishing foods."
51. Be flexible. Life is too short to worry about unmade beds.
52. Carry a notebook with you to jot down thoughts, feelings, dreams as well as jobs that need to be done.
53. Before going to sleep journal a few sentences about the day's activities.
54. Before sleep, scan your body and ask if it is well. Listen for the answer. Pay attention to any aches and pains that may need to be addressed.
55. Learn to manage change. Change is here to stay.
56. Use your evening commute as down time. Let go of work and consciously breathe. Listen to your favorite music.
57. Set clear boundaries between your work life and home life. When you can, leave work at work. Enjoy your family.
58. Before sleep, visualize your day. Bless the people that you met and the experiences that you had both good and bad.
59. Let go of your need for approval. What a drain! Every day say, "I approve of myself, and my approval of myself is the only approval that I need."
60. Set goals for yourself. Research shows that people who set goals for themselves are happier. Remember to write down your goals on paper.

61. Every day, we create order out of chaos in our lives. Plan and organize your day.
62. Identify the real priorities in your life. Move them to the top of the "to-do" list.
63. Give up needing to be Superwoman. Some things will be left undone and that is normal and okay.
64. One day a week, give up guilt. Say, "I give up feelings of guilt. Feeling guilty is not healthy for my soul."
65. Take a deep breath and affirm, "I give myself permission to slow down."
66. Accept and love the differences between your spouse and yourself.
67. Be satisfied with your achievements. Look for the positives. Be positive.
68. Find the best childcare for your child. Check references carefully.
69. Tell your children that you love them at least 3 times a day.
70. Join a support group or host one in your home.
71 Read books just for fun.
72. Consciously let go of judging yourself. At the end of the day tell yourself what a good job you've done.
73. Ask yourself, what is the best use of my time right now? Do I need to be active, or can I relax?
74. Take something off the "to-do" list. Take two or three things off the list.
75. Affirm, "I am doing the best I can."
76. It's okay to be angry. You don't need to explain. Just feel what you feel.
77. Make sure you are including time for your physical, emotional, and spiritual self.
78. Carry sticky pads with you. Jot down thoughts and then write them in a personal notebook.

79. Place a laundry basket in each bathroom for easy pick-up.
80. At work, put a note on your door or outside your cubicle that says, "Thanks for stopping by, but I'm working on a project and can't be disturbed right now. Come back at noon."
81. Use the best and most active time of day for the hardest projects. If you're a morning person, then schedule a project in the morning. If you have more energy in the afternoon, schedule a project in the afternoon.
82. Don't skip lunch! Lunchtime is your time for downtime.
83. Communicate with your supervisor or manager at work. Let them know your busy schedule at home. It might help.
84. On Sunday, check your schedule for the week. Prepare what you need to do. Delegate chores to family members. Teach them how to make their own "to-do" lists.
85. Honor the signals in your body that say you are tired. Then take some down time for yourself.
86. Always stow a hide-away key somewhere outside of the home. (Not in an obvious place.)
87. Take a few minutes to pet the dog or cat. Research confirms that petting animals can lower blood pressure.
88. It's okay to lock your bedroom door. Put a paper clock on the door that says, "Will return in 15 minutes."
89. Change your communication style. Practice assertiveness, not passivity or aggression.
90. Let others make their own decisions and learn by their own mistakes.
91. Set limits. Practice keeping the limits.
92. Get proper rest. Eat well. Exercise at something that

you like to do.

93. Find time just for yourself and do an activity that you enjoy.
94. Create a system for everyday tasks like the laundry, bills, food shopping, and cooking.
95. Anticipate a crisis. For example, what would happen if your car didn't start in the morning? Triple A service is inexpensive and it's a lifesaver in an emergency.
96. Keep extra batteries and flashlights on hand for emergencies.
97. Practice yoga. It is a wonderful, relaxing, healing tool that combines physical exercise with meditation.
98. When you're tired and can't do another thing, kick up your heels, lie back, close your eyes, and let go of everything and everybody for at least one minute. You deserve it!
99. Believe in a Higher Power of your choice. Affirm that your Higher Power is watching over you and taking care of you. There is a divine plan for your life. Align with it.
100. Be grateful for what you have. Focus on the positive as much as possible all day.

I AM Affirmations

When we say I AM statements, they generate a power-ful energy. I AM affirmations help us feel more positive and enthusiastic. In *Positive Thinking for a Time Like This*, Nor-man Vincent Peale wrote, "Every day, remind yourself of your own ability, of your good mind and affirm that you can make something really good out of your life."

Saying an affirmation everyday that begins with the words I AM begins to clear out mental blocks. When you say I AM statements, do so with consciousness, focused inten-tion, and a deliberate and positive attitude. Be conscious and energetic. At the same time, Consciously Breathe and repeat the affirmation several times. Write the affirmation down on paper and post it next to your workstation, in your car, or on the bathroom mirror. Make up your own affirmations. I AM affirmations are your personal coach. When you begin to use them, they generate energy in your life and help you feel a new sense of hope and renewal.

I AM Affirmations

1. I AM the author of my actions, my attitudes, and my experiences.
2. I love myself.
3. I AM making the most of this moment, as this is the only moment I have.
4. I AM an empowered woman.
5. I love my body.
6. I AM grateful for my present job.
7. I AM balanced, healthy, and whole.
8. I AM grateful for all of the people that I meet today.
9. I AM a risk-taker.
10. I AM enjoying life's exciting challenges.
11. I AM in charge of the thoughts that I think.
12. I AM eating wholesome and nourishing foods.
13. I AM a wonderful woman just the way that I am.
14. I AM letting go of what I cannot control.
15. I forgive myself as forgiveness opens my mind and heart to new ways of seeing others, the world, and myself.
16. I AM happy.
17. I AM letting go of negative thoughts.
18. I believe in myself.
19. I AM grateful for my spouse, partner, children, boss, and coworkers.
20. I AM a channel for God's pure light and love.
21. I AM a spokesperson for hope, renewal, and better times.

22. I know that my Higher Power supplies all the things I need in my life.
23. I AM fulfilled.
24. I AM appreciating this moment, whether at work, or walking in the park.
25. I AM certain that my future is glorious and filled with happiness and prosperity.
26. I AM prosperous.
27. I AM a good friend.
28. I AM a patient and loving parent.
29. I AM abundant. My consciousness is filled with love.
30. I AM strong.
31. I AM grateful for my ability to say "no."
32. I AM consciously creating a half-hour of down time a day just for me every day.
33. I AM choosing to be a good communicator.
34. I AM a positive thinker.
35. I AM an enthusiastic person. Every day I visualize myself as an enthusiastic person.
36. I AM a creative thinker. I am able to find creative solutions to any problem.
37. I AM letting go of fear and replacing it with faith.
38. I AM assertive. I am letting others know my needs and the way that I feel.
39. I AM making time for myself and the things I love to do.
40. I AM accepting problems as a sign of life. I am alive.
41. I AM successful.
42. I believe in myself.
43. I AM choosing to remain calm.
44. I AM remembering to take conscious breaths.
45. I AM organized. I AM choosing to let go of procrastination.
46. I AM joyful.

47. I AM managing my stress.
48. I AM containing my anger and expressing my emotions constructively.
49. I AM associating with people who nourish me.
50. I AM strong and healthy.
51. I AM visualizing myself surrounded with beautiful violet light, brilliant with color, pulsating with intensity.

About the Author

Ruth Hoskins, LCSW, BCD, Director of Relaxation International, is a clinical social worker, psychotherapist, stress management consultant, and trainer for Fortune 500 companies. She has a Master's degree from Tulane University, is a Ph.D. candidate, Board Certified Diplomate, certified relationships counselor (IRT) and approved trainer for the International Critical Incident Stress Foundation. She teaches Health Psychology, the Mind-Body-Spirit connection, and Critical Incident Stress Management (CISM) at a local college. She is the author of *Easy Stress Solutions for You* and *Active Relaxation: Five Steps to Building Self-Esteem* audios. She is available for seminars, workshops, and private consultation.

Seminars for business.

Private Instruction.

Group instruction available.

1. Meditation for Anger Management
2. Job Burnout
3. Stress and Anxiety Management.
4. Critical Incident Stress Management (CISM)
5. Wellness Workshop.
6. Meditation Instruction
7. Creating a Successful Business
8. Relationship Workshop
9. Communication Skills in Business and Home
10. Managing Change
11. Yoga in the Workplace
12. Keys to Communicating with Difficult People
13. Diversity in the Workplace
14. CPR-Consciously Preparing to Relax
15. Improving Customer Service
16. Communiating with your Teenager
17. Single Parenting
18. Balancing Work & Home Life
19. Active Relaxation
20. Making Time for Down Time
21. Animal Assisted Therapy
22. The Meaning of Dreams

Workshops can be customized for your organization.
Continuing Education Credits (CEU's) are available.

Products available through Relaxation International:

_____ Easy Stress Solutions Relaxation audio tape $12

_____ Active Relaxation audio tape available on tape and CD $15

_____ I AM a 100-MPH Woman T Shirt (specify small, medium, large) $15

Send check or money order to:
Relaxation International
Ruth Hoskins, Director
PO Box 9943
Philadelphia Pa. 19118
(Shipping $3.00)
(215) 242-6106
www.RelaxationInternational.com
Email: RelaxTraining@aol.com

Bibliography

Berger, Kathleen Strassen. *The Developing Person*. Worth Publishers, New York, 2002

Cousins, Norman. *Head First*. E.P. Dutton, New York. 1989.

Creer, Thomas L. *Psychology of Adjustment, An Applied Approach*. Prentice-Hall, 1997.

Dossey, Larry, M.D. *Reinventing Medicine Beyond Mind-Body to a New Era of Healing*. 2000.

Eliot, Robert, M.D. *From Stress to Strength.*. Bantam Books, New York, 1995.Kalat, James W. *Biological Psychology*. Wadsworth Learning Center, seventh edition, 2001.

Hoskins, Ruth. *Easy Stress Solutions for You* (audio). Relaxation International, 1999.

Hoskins & Rubin. *Active Relaxation Audio—Five Steps to More Positive Thinking*. 1998.

Hutchison, Michael. *Mega Brain*. Ballantine Books, New York, 1991.

King, Godfre Ray. *The I AM Discourses*. St. Germain Press, Inc., 1940.

Mark, Vernon, M.D., with Jeffrey P. Mark, M.Sc. *Brain Power: A Neurosurgeon's Complete Program to Maintain and Enhance Brain Fitness Throughout Your Life*. Houghton Mifflin Co., Boston, 1989.

Peale, Norman Vincent. *Positive Thinking for a Time Like This*. Prentice-Hall.

Selye, Hans. *The Stress of Life*. McGraw-Hill, 1984.

Siegel, Bernie S., M.D. *Peace, Love and Healing*. Harper Perennial, 1990.